Anonymous

An Inquiry Into the Powers of Ecclesiastics, on the Principles of Scripture and Reason

Anonymous

An Inquiry Into the Powers of Ecclesiastics, on the Principles of Scripture and Reason

ISBN/EAN: 9783337063986

Printed in Europe, USA, Canada, Australia, Japan

Cover: Foto ©ninafisch / pixelio.de

More available books at **www.hansebooks.com**

AN INQUIRY INTO THE POWERS OF ECCLESIASTICS,

ON THE PRINCIPLES OF

SCRIPTURE AND REASON.

Beware of false prophets which come to you in sheep's clothing; but inwardly they are ravening wolves.

LONDON:

PRINTED FOR J. MURRAY, NO. 32, FLEET-STREET.

MDCCLXXVI.

TO THE

PATRONS

OF

RELIGIOUS LIBERTY;

THE GENUINE FRIENDS OF CHRISTIANITY,

THE GUARDIANS OF THE MOST IMPORTANT
RIGHTS OF MANKIND,

AND THE SUREST BULWARK OF OUR
CIVIL CONSTITUTION;

THE FOLLOWING TREATISE

IS

WITH ALL POSSIBLE DEFERENCE

AND RESPECT,

INSCRIBED BY

THE AUTHOR.

PREFACE.

OF all the causes that have combined to injure the cause of Christianity, and to prevent its success; the author of the following sheets hath been long of opinion, that the pride and arrogant claims of Ecclesiastics, and the misrepresentation of certain parts of scripture to support these claims, have been none of the least considerable.

As the most effectual service, therefore, he was capable of doing to the interests of religion and society,—this little work is intended to explain, and vindicate the common rights of christianity;—to expose the false pretensions of *priests* of every denomination, and to establish the real value and importance of the ministerial character.

PREFACE.

At the same time, he is not without some apprehensions, notwithstanding the integrity of his views, and his favourable intentions to the cause which he professes to espouse; and, even amidst all that freedom of inquiry, enlargement of mind, and liberality of sentiment, by which the present age is distinguished; that so much of the *old leaven* may still remain, as to embitter the spirits of some against him as a mistaken friend, perhaps an insidious foe to it. Regardless, however, of every censure of this kind, he is not afraid to make his appeal to the judicious and candid christian. But, should he flatter his readers with the hopes of finding here any thing original, he is afraid he should only deceive himself. He assumes not the honour of being ranked among the learned or ingenious sons of science. He is a PLAIN MAN. He hath read his Bible, and thinks he hath entered into the spirit, and understands the leading design of it; and he is well pleased that by *that* spirit, and *this* design, his performance, such as it is, should be examined. Nor will he decline to be tried on the principles of reason, nor to be judged at the bar of common sense.

But,

But, though he can promife nothing original — attached to no religious party, warped by prejudices to no eftablifhed creed, and under the influence of no authority, but the authority of the fcriptures — he hath, at leaft, the merit of treading in a track wholly his own. He hath borrowed from no one. The materials are wholly drawn from his own ideas, and the beft judgement he could form from the divine record, and the malignant tendency of thofe tenets he hath attempted to overturn; and will therefore, in all probability, exhibit fome features fufficient to mark a difference, in the manner and execution, from any other who may have written on the fame fubject. And it is not impoffible, that what made fome impreffion upon his own mind, if he hath been happy enough to exprefs himfelf with perfpicuity, may have a fimilar effect upon the minds of others.

There are two objections that may occur to the defign and plan in general, which he begs leave to obviate. It may be faid that an attempt of this kind comes by far too late; that the author hath figured to himfelf pretenfions to which no order of ecclefiaftics *now* lay claim, and which no layman in his sober senses would listen to with patience, much less deliberately adopt as a part of his creed. In answer to this he will only say, that, though his observation and experience have led him to very different sentiments, he would feel a pleasure in being satisfied of the justness of this objection, more than sufficient to overbalance any little disappointment in having employed his time and attention to no purpose. The *first* would be a matter of the last importance, in his judgment, to the happiness of society, and the interests of primitive christianity; the *last* of no consideration at all.

It may, perhaps, appear to some as another objection, that the several parts of this inquiry are too detached, and seem to have too little dependence upon one another. He can offer nothing in excuse for this. A writer of more discernment and acuteness might have been able to have converted separate chapters, and to have formed the several parts, into a train of arguments issuing in one general conclusion: but he could not, without weakening, in his apprehension, the evidence upon the whole. And, perhaps, the manner of treating

ing the subject he hath pursued, may have a better effect upon the generality, little accustomed to connect distant arguments, and to estimate their combined force. He will only add, he hath done his best. If his performance hath any merit, it will be read; the publick are candid. If it hath none, let it be treated with the contempt it deserves.

AN INQUIRY INTO THE POWERS OF ECCLESIASTICS.

CHAP. I.

OF PRIESTS.

SECT. I.

OF THE STATE OF THE QUESTION.

AS the Ministers of the Christian Religion have been considered under the general denomination of *Priests*; as, for many centuries, they seem with one voice to have assumed, and, it must be acknowledged, not a few still do assume powers peculiar to that office — powers which, in the judgment of the author, never did, nor ever can, in the ordinary dispensations of Providence, belong to any mortal: to prevent mistakes, and obviate reflections that might be injurious to his real sentiments concerning the ministerial function, he begs leave to begin with explaining shortly what precise idea he affixes to this extraordinary character.

A PRIEST-

A PRIESTHOOD may be defined, in a few words, to be — an order of men appropriated by divine institution for performing certain offices in religion, which offices cannot be performed by one not thus authorised, without losing their efficacy, or that blessing with which they are supposed to be attended. Or still more explicitly — A *priesthood* is an order of men governed by certain laws, and possessed of certain privileges, independent of society, and superior to the civil, moral, or common religious rights of mankind; whose office is sacred, not from what they do, but in consequence of certain powers with which they are vested, either mediately in a fixed established order and succession, or immediately by God himself. This he apprehends is the proper idea of a *priesthood:* and such a priesthood, it is affirmed, never did exist in any age, or among any people, so far as satisfying evidence can be offered, but under the Jewish theocracy alone. He therefore who pretends that the ministerial acts which he performs, whatever their nature may be, or by whatever sacred name he may be pleased to call them — whether accounted more ordinary, or more solemn — derive their value, not from particular qualifications natural or acquired, not from decency or order, not from the station of president in a religious assembly, but from a certain mysterious connection, which is either primarily, or ultimately resolvable into a peculiar divine constitution and energy, distinct from the laws by which society is directed and governed: this man — whether he be a papist or a protestant, whether he be a minister of the church of Rome, of the church of England, or of the church of Scotland; or whether he be a professed dissenter from all establishments — is a *deceiver;* and they

they who believe his pretensions, and are under the spirit and influence of them, are, in the strictest sense, the dupes of their own credulity and superstition. It may here not be improper, however, to advertise the reader that the word *priest* is commonly used, in the following sheets, for every such claimant, or pretender to such extraordinary powers.

THIS is the arrogant and assuming character, equally injurious to the moral and civil rights of society, which the author hath attempted to expose; without one insinuation, 'tis hoped, unfriendly to the genuine ministers of religion: he can say further, that he is well disposed to make every concession that the duties of publick and social worship can possibly demand, and to acknowledge every degree of authority and respect, that publick teachers can in justice derive from thence. In order to investigate this subject as far back as possible, we shall inquire, in the first place, what light revelation, from its earliest period, gives in this question.

SECT. II.

OF THE LIGHT WHICH THE OLD TESTAMENT FURNISHES IN THIS QUESTION.

FROM the creation to the establishment of the Jewish commonwealth, the sacred record will afford us but little information with regard to the origin or nature of this institution: it being confined almost entirely to a few general hints concerning the Antediluvian world, the deluge, Noah and his family, Abraham, and

and what specially relates to his family: so that all we know of the patriarchal state, may be summed up in a few words — That in process of time it came to pass that Cain brought of the fruit of the ground an offering unto the Lord; and Abel brought also of the firstlings of his flock; that afterwards Noah, then Abraham, and lastly Jacob offered sacrifices unto the Lord — That ignorance overspread the face of the earth; the original impressions of the Deity being almost extinguished, and every corner filled with violence; so that all flesh had corrupted their ways — That to punish a world thus sunk in wickedness, an universal deluge was sent, which swept away its inhabitants: Noah and his family being alone distinguished amidst the dreadful catastrophe — That the world again multiplied, and as it multiplied, that a sense of religion again decayed — That to preserve just notions of the true God, and prevent the world from reverting into a state of total ignorance and degeneracy, Abraham was selected, a man eminent for his piety; and both he and his descendants marked as the distinguished and peculiar favourites of Heaven. This is a general view of the history of the world for two thousand years: during which period we have not one public institute with regard to any external form of religion.

From what hath been taken notice of, indeed, we are led to conclude that sacrifices and offerings made a part of the primitive religion; but in what manner, or by whom they were performed, we are left entirely in the dark. The examples before us were, certainly, personal acts of devotion. Religion wrought up into no artificial form would be very simple: and it seems probable

bable that till mankind had encreafed, every individual would be left to officiate for himfelf. But as focial worfhip, which confifts in certain external acts which all cannot perform with propriety, neceffarily fuppofes, when fociety became more numerous, that *one* muft have acted in a publick capacity as minifter or prefident, it is reafonable to think that the heads of the refpective families would be honoured with this character, or confider themfelves as naturally entitled to it, and continue to officiate as minifters within the circle of their own immediate defcendants; and that when more widely diffufed and mixed, fo that it became impoffible to join in acts of worfhip under one common head, fome idea fimilar to this would direct different focieties in their choice: that is, there would appear fome one who, by age, connections, fuperior wifdom or piety, claimed a preference. Minifters of religion, therefore, we are naturally led to fuppofe, muft have been coeval with the firft publick forms of devotion. But the divine record affords nothing, from the creation to the Abrahamic period, that can convey the moft diftant idea of a *prieft*.

LET us now inquire whether the fucceeding period, from Abraham to the commencement of the Jewifh commonwealth, furnifhes any new difcovery. And here we find two fhort anecdotes concerning this office. " And Melchifedec king of Salem brought forth bread and wine; and he was a *prieft* of the moft high God; and he bleffed him, and faid, bleffed be Abraham of the moft high God, poffeffor of heaven and earth." The hiftory of Jofeph, who feems to have been a moft political prime minifter, prefents us with the other. Concerning

cerning whom we are informed, that " when he bought the lands of Egypt for his master, only the lands of the *priests* bought he not, for the *priests* had a portion assigned them by Pharaoh, and did eat of the portion which Pharaoh gave them; wherefore they sold not their lands." This is all the light that can be derived from the sacred history, and which can avail nothing by way of precedent. For with regard to Melchisedec, as the short hint given by the historian can lead us to nothing certain concerning the nature of his office, or the extent of his priestly powers; from the further accounts given of him (which is all we know of the matter) by the penman of the hundred and tenth psalm, and the author of the epistle to the Hebrews, it evidently appears that he was a priest of so extraordinary a nature, that we cannot so much as form any idea of it; except in general, that he is exhibited as a striking type of the great high priest over the house of God, and therefore can bear no similitude to any settled order of priesthood. And with regard to the Egyptian *priests*, it is sufficient to observe, that they were the ministers of the grossest superstition and idolatry, of whose powers or succession we know nothing.

One thing, however, we may learn from this story, that an order of men thus distinguished, and who had acquired such credit with the state, as to have lands assigned to them, and besides a daily portion of meat from Pharaoh, had not attained to this influence all at once. It seems rather to have been the work of time; and consequently that their origin is to be traced much higher; though it is impossible to affirm any thing with certainty

Chap. I. OF PRIESTS.

tainty on a subject, where the only record that could give us any information is entirely silent. From this silence, however, the presumption is, that, at whatever time, or from whatever causes, the office of a *priest* became venerable among the nations; this institution, as peculiarly confined to an established order essentially distinct from the people, holding a commission, and possessed of powers not merely human, had not yet received the divine sanction.

It may be said, that it did not fall in with the design of the historian to give an account of things at large, but only some general out-line introductory to the establishment of the family of Abraham. That this is the chief view of the sacred writer, is readily admitted; but, as Moses wrote more probably from immediate revelation, than from any traditions that might have been preserved in the family of Abraham—it being far from probable that divine wisdom should rest the authority of an original record upon tradition—it being even absurd to suppose tradition of any kind a solid ground of divine faith through successive ages, as it is hoped will appear with decisive evidence afterwards——as Moses, therefore, wrote from immediate revelation, it is difficult to conceive that God should have made any discovery to the first inhabitants of the earth, concerning an institution of such importance to mankind, as the nature and extent of the priestly class and powers; and at the same time, that, in a subsequent revelation to be committed to writing, containing every thing from the creation downwards, and designed to remain as a standing original record, not one hint should have been given concerning

cerning such an institution. The Almighty was now about to establish a real priesthood; to delegate an order of men honoured with singular powers, where his authority and the signal interpositions of his providence were to be visible to all; and where the evidence of the divine sanction depended not on the bold asseverations of designing men. If a similar institution had ever obtained, is it probable that we should have had no notice concerning it; how long its authority remained, when and where it had been corrupted, and in what respects the first institution was the same, or different from the subsequent one? The silence of the historian, therefore, we may hold a presumption, not a *feeble*, but a *strong* one, that the priesthood, as limited by divine appointment to an exclusive order of men, had not, till the commencement of the Jewish Theocracy, received the divine sanction. But, admitting that Moses had his information wholly from tradition, can we suppose that a tradition which had preserved an account of facts seemingly trivial in their nature, should have failed in transmitting an account of one professedly of the highest importance, of an institution of such universal concern? Could Noah have been ignorant of it? or would he, as a preacher of righteousness, and in whose family the sole powers of priesthood, after the deluge, must have remained — would he, it is asked, have neglected to perpetuate such an establishment agreeably to the divine appointment and model? or could such an appointment and model, established after the flood, have been forgotten by Abraham and his descendants, among whom it must have been particularly observed? or finally, could the order and succession of priesthood have been

known

known and observed by them as a sacred institution, and no notice have been taken of it by the historian? Admitting therefore, that Moses had his information from tradition, we are, on all the principles of probability, in other words, led to the same conclusion — that Levi and his sons were the first who could claim the honour of priesthood.

SECT. III.

OF THE IMPROBABILITY OF PRESERVING AN INSTITUTION OF PRIESTHOOD WITHOUT A WRITTEN RECORD.

IT may not be improper to investigate this subject a little further, by enquiring what was most likely to be the state of things, upon the supposition that the most rational forms of religious worship, and a regular order of priests had been instituted by immediate divine appointment, but without any written record to which a constant and unerring appeal could have been made. The question then is, could such an institution have been preserved, so as to enable us to judge with any certainty, or to give sufficient satisfaction to the human mind concerning the divine origin of it, and its real similitude to its antient form; what innovations might have been introduced, or what changes it might have undergone? The probability certainly is, that it could not. It is morally impossible it should. Positive institutions are subjected to innovations from a thousand causes, which, if they are not sufficient to change their nature altogether, make them something so different from their original form, that you cannot without the utmost difficulty mark any likeness. Even those truths that are supposed to have been originally discovered by revelation, though agreeable to the natural feelings of the human mind, and founded on the soundest deductions of reason, cannot be transmitted through successive generations without a perfect standard to which we can appeal, but with the utmost danger of being greatly perverted, if not totally lost. From the accounts of the Antediluvian age, it seems self-evident that the most perfect oral instruction affords but very imperfect grounds of probability; that is, while persons still living, and of undoubted veracity, could attest the facts, and carry down through many centuries what they themselves had been eye and ear witnesses of; while they could unite the knowledge and experience of seven, eight, or nine hundred years as a direction to those who were, more or less, their cotemporaries. When, under such circumstances of advantage, tradition proved utterly inadequate for preserving just notions of God and his worship; what are we to look for afterwards—when human life became diminished to a span, when God confounded the language of men, and scattered them abroad upon the face of the earth—but fable and absurdity? If at this period, the wickedness of men had become so great, that on this account, the inhabitants of the earth were driven as vagabonds without union, and incapable of intercourse, so that they could not assist one another in forming, or transmitting one common or religious theory; what must have been the state of the world in the course of succeeding ages, supposing an

original

original institution of priesthood immediately appointed by God, or handed down from Noah — that the administration of certain sacred rites and ordinances, and the performance of certain offices had been committed to a particular family, or one order of men exclusive of all others? It may be affirmed, on all the principles of probability, that if any traditions had remained concerning such an institution, they must have been so vague and imperfect; they must have been traced amidst so many absurdities, and even impieties; as to render it impossible, without a new discovery, to have established upon this foundation any confident ritual or external form of worship. Nature alone — what principles of reason remained uncorrupted in the human mind — could have been consulted with safety, without deriving the least advantage from this supposed original discovery and institution.

It hath been admitted, that, from observing almost among all nations a ritual, however differing in others, agreeing in the common points of priest and sacrifice, the mind would be naturally led to think, that sacrifices had constituted a part of the antient religion, and that an order of men, called priests, had had a certain department in the public religious service. But, from having seen an Egyptian or Carthaginian priest; or having witnessed the vain and ridiculous, or the immoral, the unnatural, the barbarous rites themselves, and their public worship, as well as the homage to their deities; would it have been possible to have formed any idea of what a priest was before the flood? Could one have figured, it is asked, what, at the days of Babel, their public ritual was, or in what manner it was conducted?

ducted? To what tribe the order of *priesthood* belonged, in what manner priests were installed, what precise department they held, or what authority belonged to them? The one certainly could lead him to no idea of the other. The fact is, a few positive precepts perhaps excepted, the first inhabitants of the earth seem to have been left to the original impressions of nature, which, by proper attention, were sufficient to have directed to every necessary mode of worship: or if any particular revelation was originally vouchsafed, we have no intimation concerning it, except so far as relates to the grand promise of the *seed of the woman*. While this was kept in remembrance, and understood, nothing further was necessary.

SECT. IV.

Of the natural suggestions of the human mind on this subject.

IT is impossible, perhaps, to affirm with absolute certainty concerning the feelings and operations of the human mind in a state greatly dissimilar to our own: and yet we cannot suppose a reasonable and moral being in circumstances, in which we do not naturally figure to ourselves, what ideas it must unavoidably form of its dependence and obligation, what hopes and fears must occupy its mind; and our conclusions in every case of this kind, are not deduced from mere theory or abstract reasoning, but from an analogy in the human mind, that seems immediately to lead us to judge, from a comparison

parison with ourselves. Thus, if we suppose the first inhabitants of the earth to have been impressed, whether from the internal frame of their own minds, or from revelation, with a sense of deity, the beneficent author of nature, the moral and righteous governor of the world; while such impressions remained, they would naturally be accompanied with correspondent feelings; they would fill the heart with chearful gratitude and humble hope; gratitude from a sense of dependence and obligation; hope founded on the benignity and goodness manifested so conspicuously in the whole order of nature, in life, and the various blessings of it, and which they had not altogether rendered themselves unworthy of. These would appear to be the feelings of the human mind in a state where the moral powers were not greatly depraved. And while we could suppose mankind to remain in this state, religion, with regard to the external mode of it, would, no doubt, be very plain:—divested of every artificial ornament, and confined to a few obvious expressions of gratitude and devotion; or the simple observance of any religious rite the Almighty might appoint, or any public service that social worship might require. There would be no occasion for an order of *priests*; no one amidst the purity of such impressions, and such just and rational views of religion, would think of such a character. A spiritual worship rises superior to every idea of this kind, and rejects every intermediate human office, except what public order and decency may render expedient, or necessary.—But when did this state exist, wherein the moral powers were not greatly depraved? From the creation to the translation of Enoch, I should apprehend, containing a space of

almost

almost a thousand years. As we can hardly suppose that the fall, whatever, upon the whole, might be the natural or moral consequences of it, would deface the original features of the human mind, or obscure any revelation concerning God and religious duty, so far as to leave no certain rule of conduct; we are naturally led to think, to whatever degree of wickedness individuals may have arrived, that the original impressions of divinity would not, all at once, be erased from the soul of man; and that with regard to communities, or distinct tribes, a sense of moral obligation, and of the duties of natural religion in general, would diminish gradually. The scriptures no where lead the mind to a rapid transition from the state of perfection, in knowledge and virtue, in which Adam was created, to the extremeties of ignorance and vice. Those seeds of corruption, which were by sin introduced into his natural and moral constitution, operated by gradual and progressive steps: in the one they issued in death, in the other in universal ignorance and depravity of manners.

But without insisting upon this, let us suppose mankind in a different state,—in a state of ignorance, degeneracy, and guilt; this very feeling, the source of devotion, gratitude, and hope, would produce a contrary effect—a slavish fear and dread of the Deity, from the apprehensions of having exposed ourselves to his just displeasure: and the mind, under the influence of gross misconceptions of the Divinity, and distressed with gloomy apprehensions of impending justice; or desirous to obtain certain blessing, or to avert certain evils, without knowing in what manner it shall proceed, will be infallibly

infallibly led to some external ritual, more or less absurd according to its external complexion, the prejudices by which it may be influenced, and the ideas of that Supreme Power which it hath offended. But as man come to lose sight of the spiritual nature of religion, and substitute an external ritual in the place of it, which is supposed to render us acceptable to the Deity, the person employed in performing those ceremonies, or officiating in those forms, in which this ritual may consist, will grow into a sort of veneration, and be deemed sacred; and the divine efficacy which is thought to accompany them, will either be gradually transferred to him, or be considered as inseparably connected with his office. Now, a veneration founded on ignorance and fear will naturally encrease. Superstition and credulity know no bounds; and a power in religion, being the supreme power, will be artfully preserved, and studiously improved. The multitude, influenced by custom, and governed by authority, would quickly submit to any establishment which would make their consciences easy, and, at the same time, leave them in quiet possession of their favourite pursuits. The holy fraternity, led good by interest and ambitious views, under various pretences, would assume new rights, and extend their dominion over the consciences of their simple, ignorant, votaries. The Deity would be represented as too pure to hold immediate communication with profane worshippers, and, therefore, accessible only through the intermediate offices of his holy ministers.—And thus their decisions would become sacred; few being able to investigate the truth, and fewer daring to dispute with an order of men, now

supposed

supposed to be possessed of certain unalienable divine powers.

In this manner alone, in a state of general corruption, would ignorance and superstition—a slavish fear of the Deity, arising from a sense of guilt, without a proper discovery of his moral perfections—operate on the mind, and lay the foundation of all that spiritual jurisdiction, and unlimited usurpation, over the consciences of men, which the pride or policy of *priests* have hitherto aimed at, or possessed. One step would lead to another.—Now become necessary and venerable by their profession, they would think of enlarging their sphere of action, and by gradual advances would assume a direction in civil, as well as religious concerns; it being almost impossible to separate these two.—He to whom I have submitted my understanding and conscience, without reserve, in matters of greater concern, will think himself entitled to advise and direct me in those of lesser; and by yielding up the leading faculties of my mind, I have left myself no capacity of resistance, should he who pretends to advise and direct me, insist on absolute obedience; because he has it always in his power to make a last and decisive appeal to that faculty which I have already resigned to him, and which is the supreme and final judge.—And in this manner things would probably go on, whether on the plan of natural or revealed religion, if we suppose that the one or the other is greatly corrupted, till, by some extraordinary interposition of Providence, the minds of men should become enlightened, the knowledge of our duty as rational and moral agents, and that worship which is acceptable to the Deity should be clearly exhibited;

bited; and the minds of men opened to impartial inquiry, and set free from every unnatural restraint.

How far this description is a natural representation of the progress of the human mind, from its first feelings, to the establishment of a public ritual, and external mode of worship, of the origin and usurpation of *priests*, and of the veneration they have acquired in every age from their deluded votaries, is readily submitted to those who can judge with propriety, and censure with candour. To some it may appear wholly chimerical. It may be so. They will be good enough, however, to point out some more probable origin of that establishment we have endeavoured to search for, so far as the antient record, and attention to the human mind could direct us. To others it may appear just, but drawn rather from experience, and what hath been observed, in fact, among the nations, than from any antecedent principles characteristic of our natures. That what we have here supposed to be the natural progress of the human mind, is agreeable to fact, and what experience hath every where discovered, where a *priesthood* hath been established amidst universal ignorance and corruption of manners, is admitted: but it seems no less certain, that the principles taken notice of would produce the same effects, and, therefore, afford the most probable account that can be given of what experience and observation confirm.

SECT.

SECT. V.

OF THE DESIGN OF THE JEWISH PRIESTHOOD, AND THE NECESSITY OF A NEW REVELATION TO FIX OUR IDEAS ON THIS SUBJECT.

IT must be acknowledged that other causes, besides an immediate discovery from God fixing a standard of duty and worship, might combine to introduce a change in a national system of religion. An ambitious political prince, raised above religious scruples, might mount the throne, choose to limit the powers of ecclesiastics, and touch their coffers: a people might be conquered, and obliged to receive their religion and laws from the point of the sword: amidst civil commotions, certain concessions might be made, where different parties had been struggling with one another : or, amidst the progress of science, a ray of light might possibly dart forth, owing to different natural or political causes, and point out some of the more absurd or pernicious opinions, or more gross and ridiculous rites and practices. But, upon the whole, it may be affirmed, that whatever change might happen, would be a change, at best, but of one foolery or absurdity for another. Ecclesiastics would either keep or regain their hold; and the minds of the multitude would be gradually prepared for new usurpations. It is a fixed standard alone, bearing the certain marks of divinity, that can prove sufficient to ascertain, with precision and authority, the boundaries between civil and ecclesiastical powers, the claims of *priests*, and the religious rights of mankind. That certain circumstances may

unite

unite to divert the attention of men, even from such a standard, and render it the means by which ecclesiastics may assume that very power which it disclaims, experience will not permit us to doubt; but while itself remains uncorrupted, there are still hopes, that, amidst every partial and temporary imposition, the human mind will be brought back again to its native vigour, and to vindicate its genuine rights.

There are only two religious systems, that can lay claim, with any probable degree of evidence, to divine authority—the Old and the New Testaments. The first hath been examined to the date of the Jewish theocracy; and it is presumed, that a very little attention to that religious theory will easily satisfy the mind, that it could not be designed for perpetuity, nor can possibly be established into a model. It was a system of a very peculiar and extraordinary nature; intended, in the *first* place, to preserve the descendants of Abraham from the idolatry of the nations, and thus to maintain the purity of the worship of the true God, and the essential duties of religion. Now, for this purpose, it was necessary that their public ritual should bear as near a resemblance as possible, without partaking of their folly or inhumanity, to the forms to which they had been accustomed, and which still surrounded them on all sides. They would have been immediately shocked by the appearance of a religion that had left nothing to strike their senses, or to correspond with their former ideas. But while the same externals were exhibited, of temple and altar, of priest and sacrifice, they would be more easily reconciled to what might appear to them but lesser differences.

differences.—But, besides preserving them from idolatry by a similarity of externals; by the frequent and signal interpositions of the ALMIGHTY, by which he appeared to act as the supreme magistrate in their commonwealth, added to the majesty and glory of his house, and the distinguishing splendour and power of his ministers, the minds of the people were overawed with a just and abiding sense of the divinity; the name of JEHOVAH, as the true God, was made known among the heathens; and a counter-part to *their* worship was publicly and solemnly exhibited, that rendered all their idolatrous and superstitious machinery mean and contemptible, and that infinitely outdid every pretension of their *lying priests*.— Thus, the nations were made to fear and stand in awe, their deceiving ministers were confounded, and an early light appeared in the East, sufficient, at least, to lead those who were willing to be directed by it, to just notions of God and their duty.

But the New Testament gives us, in the *second* place, a key that opens to a new view, and throws a light upon the darkest parts of this dispensation. It informs us, that the whole ceremonial was typical, "that the tabernacle was a figure, for the time present, which stood in carnal ordinances imposed on them till the time of reformation, and which could not make them that did the service perfect as pertaining to the conscience:"— That in *itself* the whole ritual was to be considered as *beggarly elements*,—but as pointing at the future designs of Providence, *richly fraught* with *spiritual* blessings:— That it was designed not only for preserving just notions of the true God, but likewise a deep sense of guilt, for the

the expiating of which one was to appear in the end of the world — at once both the prieſt and the ſacrifice. " For the law was added becauſe of tranſgreſſion, till the ſeed ſhould come to whom the promiſe was made."— That, therefore, in the perſon of JESUS OF NAZARETH, who is " the end of the law to them that believe," the whole terminated as plainly expreſſed by an Apoſtle, — " When theſe things were *thus* ordained, the prieſts went always into the firſt tabernacle accompliſhing the ſervice of God; but into the ſecond went the high prieſt alone, once every year, not without blood, which he offered for himſelf and the errors of the people — but Chriſt being come an high prieſt of good things to come, by a greater and more perfect tabernacle, not made with hands — by his own blood entered in *once* into the holy place, having obtained eternal redemption for us." *Prieſts*, and ſacrifices, and altars, therefore, are no more. " Our fathers worſhipped in this *mountain*, and in *Jeruſalem* ye ſay is the place where men ought to worſhip — Jeſus ſaith, Believe me, the hour cometh, and now is, when ye ſhall neither worſhip in this *mountain*, nor yet at *Jeruſalem* ; but when the true worſhippers ſhall worſhip the father in *ſpirit* and in *truth*." Thus, it is demonſtratively evident, that we have nothing to do with this diſpenſation, with the order of its prieſts, or the forms of its worſhip. Its whole value reſts on the importance of the evidence it furniſhes for its own diſſolution — the fulfillment of the types, and the accompliſhment of the prophecies in the perſon of JESUS, which prove that he is the CHRIST. For with regard to what is moral, it reſts upon its own foundation,

dation, it is of perpetual obligation, and must be the same under every divine dispensation.

To the religion of Christ, therefore, we must appeal. We have no other law or directory. Here we must learn, if there is any external mode of worship prescribed, what rites and ceremonies are peculiar to it, how far they bind the conscience, and are of a perpetual nature; if an order of *priesthood* is established, with what powers they are entrusted, and what is the extent of their commission; whether in religion every thing is personal, and the right of every individual, at least till it is by common consent transferred to one or more; or whether, with regard to certain acts necessary to salvation, we must depend upon the intermediate ministry of others, to whom the exclusive right of performing them is committed by an immediate divine institution. These are questions, surely, of the highest and most serious concern. To throw some light, therefore, on a subject of such infinite importance, is the design of the following chapters. And to pave the way, by setting aside every adventitious authority, it will be necessary to shew, that the Scriptures are the only rule of faith, and can have no dependence on any human traditions.

CHAP. II.

OF TRADITION.

SECT I.

Of the importance of the question.

IT may be thought, perhaps, that the question concerning tradition, is a question with the papists only; but this would be a mistake; though even in this point of view, it would not cease to be a question of great importance, considering the growth of popery in these kingdoms, for almost a century past, and that a decision of this single point, without descending to particulars, would go well nigh to shake the foundation of this formidable fabric. For, as clear as noon day, if the Scriptures are a perfect and exclusive rule of faith, popery rests its distinguishing doctrines on a false bottom, and is a most presumptuous imposition upon the faith of christians. But, setting popery aside from the question, whoever is at the pains to attend to the nature of several tenets, opinions, and usages, maintained by protestants, and by which they have exposed their cause to the same objections from every sober and impartial inquirer, with popery itself, will immediately perceive, that they derive their weight, not from the Scriptures, not from the reason of the human mind, but from a very different source — from antiquity: that is, from the practice of what they are pleased to call the primitive church, from the writings of some venerable father, or from the decision of some national or general council: in short, from some quarter or other, which, in the last resort, may be properly resolved into human authority.

From whatever cause it ariseth, there seems to be in the minds of men some secret misgivings, that the New Testament is not a foundation, broad and secure enough to rest their faith wholly on; and till these misgivings are fairly removed, by establishing the authority of the Scriptures, as a perfect and infallible rule of faith, independent upon every tradition, every practice, however hoary with age, or venerable from custom — independent upon every human doctrine, though supported by the greatest authority on earth; we shall never be disposed to pay them that reverence which they deserve, nor to commit our cause wholly to them. But bring men once to place unlimited confidence in the Divine Record; emancipate the mind fairly from the shackles of human authority, and the word of God would run and be glorified; credulity would be converted into rational inquiry, superstition and ridiculous forms into liberal devotion, and every traditionary doctrine, or practice, introduced as an essential part of religion, would be treated as a base design to lessen the credit of the authenticated canon, and to enslave the consciences of men, by substituting in the place of it an usurped authority.—Some observations, therefore, upon this subject, are humbly offered to the reader, which, if they are not necessary to those to whom it may appear sufficiently plain, it is hoped, will be excused for the sake of others, who may have bestowed less attention upon it.

SECT. II.

OF THE DESIGN OF COMMITTING THE SACRED ORACLES TO WRITING.

IT deserves particular attention in this disquisition, that the great design of committing the sacred oracles to writing was, not merely to be a standard to which the age in which they were written might appeal, but every succeeding age. They seem particularly designed in this *latter* view; because the christians, to whom the inspired writers address themselves, are every where supposed to be well acquainted with the distinguishing facts, and doctrines of their religion; those at Rome excepted, to whom, therefore, the Apostle saw it necessary to give an account of christianity more at large, as a system which they had, yet, but an imperfect knowledge of. He writes not to admonish, or put them in mind of doctrines that had been formerly taught and explained to them, but to inform them of things of which hitherto they seem to have been, in a great measure, ignorant: but, at the same time, he expresses himself with a freedom and confidence, which evidently arose, from the full knowledge and conviction, that the doctrines which he explains and enforces were generally believed, and, at the same time, received among christians. The design of the written record, therefore, was chiefly to be a perfect and permanent standard, by which the body of christians might be enabled to judge, with certainty, between doctrines revealed, and authorised by God, and every human pretension, to the end of the world. This conclusion cannot be got over, but upon one or other of these suppositions — That the sacred penmen were not, at the time of writing, sufficiently instructed in the christian system — That they had forgotten some things of importance, which they afterwards called to their remembrance, and delivered orally to be transmitted by tradition — or, that they judged tradition a manner of conveying facts, and doctrines, equally certain; and, in every future age, as much to be depended upon, as committing them to writing. Let us examine into each of these.

WITH regard to the *first*, then, there can be no doubt. The sacred writers were fully instructed. They were with their Lord on all occasions, they saw all his miracles, they heard all his discourses; and they had opportunity to be thoroughly satisfied by after-inquiry, where through their own weakness and prejudices, they could not readily enter into the spirit, or perceive the design, tendency, or extent of his doctrines. Before his departure from them, he opened their understanding, that they should understand the Scriptures; and was seen of them, after his resurrection, forty days speaking of the things that pertain to the kingdom of God. — The Apostle Paul, who writes more than all the other Apostles, not being a fellow attendant with the other disciples on their Lord, was called afterwards, in an extraordinary manner, and immediately taught from heaven. — The Apostles, therefore, had every advantage

tage neceffary to a knowing and faithful difcharge of their office.

Nor, in the *fecond* place, was it poffible for them to have forgotten the divine inftructions they received, " The Comforter, which is the Holy Ghoft, which the Father will fend in my name, he fhall teach you all things, and bring all things to your remembrance, whatfoever I have faid unto you." So that had they been partially inftructed during their Lord's continuance with them, they were afterwards under the guidance of the unerring fpirit of knowledge and truth.

If any thing, then, of importance to be known was omitted, it muft of neceffity, in the *laft* place, have been owing to *this* — that thofe facred writers were of opinion, that this *omiffion* might be fupplied with equal certainty and advantage by *tradition*. This is the capital point, and on which, it fhould appear, that the final decifion of this queftion muft reft. — And *here* an attempt fhall be made, from every reafon that can fatisfy the human mind, to prove that the infpired penmen neither did, nor could have intended fuch a manner of conveyance.

SECT. III.

OF THE ABSURDITY OF SUPPOSING A DOUBLE RULE OF FAITH—ONE WRITTEN—THE OTHER TRADITIONAL.

IT will be allowed, on all hands, that to deliver doctrines, or an account of facts and tranfactions orally, is by far more eafy than to commit them to writing: so that he who sits down to write a book or epistle containing such doctrines, facts, or transactions, must be supposed to do it under this conviction — that the method he pursues is necessary for preserving the memory, and transmitting to future ages a just narrative, and an impartial account of them. Now, it will be likewise admitted, that men calling themselves the apostles of Jesus Christ, have committed to writing the transactions of his life, besides other facts and doctrines of the highest importance. In this case, they either did consider writing as a more certain manner of conveyance than tradition, or, I desire to know, why they came to write at all? Their time seems to have been but ill employed, if, with greater ease to themselves, and equal security to mankind, they might have committed the whole into the bosom of the *church*, by her to have been faithfully communicated to her implicit sons. — It seems, at least, difficult to justify the conduct of the sacred penmen, if tradition is to be considered as on a foot with writing. They, certainly ought, either to have written nothing at all, or to have written the whole: nothing, if tradition can give equal assurance to the human mind with a written record: the whole, if writing is not only the best security, but the only credible evidence. Their having committed any thing at all to writing, therefore, is a moral demonstration, that they have committed the whole, and trusted nothing to another channel. Let it not be said, that the Apostles might have, occasionally, delivered things orally to certain christian societies, to whom they have not written at all: for what the Apostles *might* have done we know not, but so far as we are informed of what they did. But supposing the fact, would

would they have delivered to one society of christians doctrines or practices of universal obligation, which they had, in no part of their writings to the other churches, taken notice of? Were the many to submit to the authority of the few? Were the churches to whom the Apostles had particularly written, to take a report, at second hand, from others to whom they had not written at all?— Or could the infallible inspired preachers seriously intend to bind the consciences of the christians to whom they wrote, and the consciences of christians in every future age, by doctrines, practices, or institutes of any kind, without one intimation in all their epistles, that they had done so, in what manner they were to be transmitted, what were their importance and obligation, and what marks of credibility they were to carry in them? On the answer to these questions we might rest the decision of this argument; but as it is a capital one, and it is hoped will appear plain, at the same time, to every reader, we beg leave to explain our ideas, and throw a little light further upon it, by the following plain illustration.

Let us put the case, then, that one writes a book to preserve the memory of some recent transaction, or some important discovery to mankind; but wherein certain things are of design omitted, no less important and necessary to be known than those with which the public is made acquainted; nay, without which the knowledge of every other discovery or transaction would be imperfect.—That, in order to supply this defect, the author did intend, at the time of writing, another channel of conveyance, and had actually committed the secret to a select

select few, by them to be communicated to the public at discretion; without one restriction as to time, place, or manner. On this supposition, what opinion should we form of the writer? That he was a fool, or a knave, beyond all doubt: most probably that he was a knave; and that, whatever he might pretend, or whatever apology his friends might offer for him, he had something farther in view than to establish a faithful repository for the public.—That there must have been a serious and deliberate design of putting something into the hands of favourites, of which they might avail themselves:—That their interest was more at heart with him than the benefit of the public; and, rather than frustrate this end, he was willing to risque the abuse, if not the total loss, of this discovery to mankind. Who, possessed of the least degree of discernment, would hesitate a moment in pronouncing such a writer, be who he will, a designing knave?—Or, put the case, that one should send a letter to a friend, informing him of matters of great importance, in which he was immediately and nearly interested, and this with all the attention and warmth that honest zeal could possibly inspire; and yet, without giving one hint concerning it in his whole letter, should intend to trust the bearer with many things of great consequence relative to the same subject, and, without which, the letter could not answer the intention of the writer with regard to the capital information designed by it;—nay more, without the interpretation of the bearer, that the letter itself could not possibly be understood: what judgment, it is asked, would any man of common sense deliver upon it?—That the writer was a fool:—he could deliver no other. And yet who does not

not see that your traditionary pretences throw the same imputation of knavery or folly on the sacred writers?—Here is a record, supposed to be divine, written on purpose to preserve the memory of the most important transactions; a discovery of facts and doctrines, of infinitely more concern to mankind than any human discovery whatever.—The New Testament is a letter from Christ, and his Apostles, concerning a new and gracious scheme of salvation to guilty men; who are addressed with all the attention to their spiritual concerns, all the importunity and fervour of spirit that the fulness of divine affection can possibly express; who are instructed, admonished, and, in particular, are guarded against deceivers and false spirits pretending to *another* gospel; and yet by this claim to tradition, they are supposed to have left both doctrines and practices necessary to salvation, to be published, at second hand, and to be transmitted orally through successive generations: they are supposed to have written things by halves, and then to have established trustees for supplying their defects. This would be such an imperfection in the Apostolic writings, and render them a rule of faith so precarious, as must necessarily lessen our esteem, if not strike at the credit of them altogether.

SECT. IV.

OF THE IMPERFECTION AND UNCERTAINTY OF TRADITION IN GENERAL, AS A GROUND OF CREDIBILITY.

THE practice of all civilized nations is sufficient to convince us, that they have judged tradition a channel

channel no ways adequate for tranſmitting hiſtory, ſcience, or law; becauſe no event of any importance, no diſcovery of any benefit to mankind, no laws formed to regulate ſociety have been, in fact, left to reſt on ſo precarious a foundation. No ſooner do we find a people emerging from a ſtate of ignorance and barbariſm; no ſooner doth the dawn of knowledge and improvement appear, than we perceive the hiſtorical page beginning to unfold itſelf, and ſome public code, however imperfect, to be eſtabliſhed — facts collected from the beſt traditional authority — laws that depended on cuſtom alone, converted into a written common law, with ſuch alterations and additions as appeared, at that time, neceſſary for the publick ſecurity and happineſs. Or if cuſtoms obtain in any country that ſtill have the force of law, and are conſidered as a ſupplement to the public code, they are ſuch as appear not inconſiſtent with the written law, and by univerſal precedent are ſo fixed and explained, in every poſſible caſe, that they cannot be miſtaken. No wiſe people, where the uſe of letters had been known, ever did, or could think of leaving laws, upon which the public order and utility depended, to be handed down by tradition; much leſs is there a caſe to be found, where they have committed to writing certain laws, and left others of equal importance to be tranſmitted orally to poſterity; ſtill leſs, where they have been entruſted into the hands of a few, with an excluſive privilege of explaining and declaring what their nature, extent, and obligation ſhould be; who from every motive of intereſt and ambition that could bias the human mind, would be led to impoſe upon the public.

As the laws of all civilized nations being committed to writing is a demonstration, on the one hand, that they had judged tradition an imperfect and uncertain manner of conveyance; on the other, the fables and absurd theology, the unconnected facts, the marvellous, and incredible abounding in every nation, where, either the art of writing had been unknown, or uncultivated, is a demonstration no less clear, that little or no credit is to be given to the most perfect accounts transmitted this way. Experience will enable us to bring the matter still nearer home, and within a narrower compass. It will shew us, that evidence, even at first hand, when men are under the power of prejudices, or have any interest to deceive, deserves but little credit: nay, which is more inexplicable, it will show that, where there can be no prospect of interest, no prejudices arising from ill will or opposition, there appears in the human mind a strong propensity to falsify, to invert, to add, to diminish, or to throw a false gloss over the plainest facts; so that seldom the same story is told the same way, though it hath happened in our time, — yesterday, — in our very neighbourhood. Upon what principles, then, are we to conclude that credit is due to tales that have passed through the hands of thousands, all having a common interest to deceive? or, supposing that they have been told the same way immemorially, how shall we trace them to their original, or arrive at any certainty concerning the authenticity of them? neither the consistency of a story in itself, nor its antiquity, nor both, are a sufficient ground of credibility, without being further ascertained when it was first broached, and by whom: what evidence, at that time, was laid before the public, and in what

what manner it was received, and came to acquire credit — and this we may venture to say, with regard to traditions, in general, and with regard to the traditions in question, in particular, is impossible. Let us, even, suppose that we could tell the persons by their names, characters, and places of abode, who pretend first to have received traditions from the apostles, or from others who had received them from the apostles at first, second, or third hand; or by revelation immediately — let us suppose that we could precisely say, where, when, and by whom this or that tradition was first ushered into the light, and under pretence of what authority; it would all amount to nothing as a rule of faith, which must ultimately rest on the divine record either immediately, as to what it contains, or mediately, by authorising us to transfer our faith, in particular circumstances, to human authority — especially if we add that all ecclesiastical traditions are so distant from, so inconsistent with the spirit of Christianity, and so entirely calculated to aggrandize the *Church*, that they exhibit a stronger internal evidence of their being spurious — the artful fabrication of *priests*, than could arise from every other argument.

SECT. III.

OF THE ABUSE WITH REGARD TO DOCTRINES AND PRACTICES IN THE PRIMITIVE AGES OF CHRISTIANITY.

WHAT hath been advanced under the foregoing section will appear with additional evidence, if we observe, that in the very times of the apostles themselves, no small part of the churches they had planted, instead of being pure and faithful repositories of the precious truths they had been carefully instructed in, was become infected with the most futile conceits, and most dangerous errors; and, on the apostolic foundation, had reared up a heterogeneous superstructure of pagan, and Jewish materials. No admonitions, though under the immediate eye of one or other of these extraordinary ministers, could preserve them from corrupting the simplicity of the gospel. If they had been converted from Judaism, with what difficulty were they brought to depart from circumcision, from meats, from drinks, from holy days, and new moons, and this after their errors and danger were repeatedly set before them? Many who professed Christianity, after every remonstrance adhered obstinately to these, and maintained them with greater zeal and strictness than its most distinguishing and important doctrines. If from heathenism—the same propensity appeared in adopting pagan tenets, and conforming to their modes of worship; feasting in their temples, eating things offered to idols, and a voluntary humility in worshipping angels. "Stand fast in the liberty wherewith Christ hath made you free, and be not entangled again in the yoke of bondage. Behold I Paul say unto you, that if ye be circumcised Christ shall avail you nothing; for I testify to every man that is circumcised that he is a debtor to the whole law — How turn ye to weak and beggarly elements, ye observe days, and months, and times, and years; I am afraid of you, lest I have bestowed labour in vain — I marvel that ye are so soon removed into another gospel — Let no man beguile you of your reward in a voluntary humility and worshipping of angels — The things that the gentiles sacrifice, they

sacrifice

sacrifice unto idols, and I would not that ye should have fellowship with devils. — Flee from idolatry." Now, if it was so difficult to preserve the first churches under the influence, even, of an extraordinary dispensation of Providence, and the immediate direction of infallible guides, from dangerous errors both in doctrine and practice, what was to be looked for when *they* were gone ? Where the unhappy influences of a spirit of prejudice, novelty, and innovation had already so remarkably appeared; what was to be looked for but that the written record itself, however plain and definitive with regard to every article of faith and duty, would prove insufficient to correct, and restrain such a disposition ? — That notions and tenets would be broached and propagated, and particular rites, practices and usages, supported by certain explications of scripture, with which in fact they had no concern, or by apostolic practice and authority would be recommended ; wherein one society of christians would differ from another, according to the notions and views of their respective leaders. As this is what might have been looked for, from minds under the prepossession of so different, and often contradictory religious tenets, before their conversion to christianity ; such were in reality the effects, immediately to be taken notice of, which early appeared among the christian sectaries ; among whom we observe so much *arrogance* and *enthusiasm*, on the one hand, so much *credulity* and *superstition*, on the other, that those only, who have read the history of the first centuries can believe it. I shall present the reader, unacquainted with this subject, with an example of both.

THE

Chap. II. OF TRADITION.

The divine Ignatius shall furnish the *first*, where the inquisitive may find a curious specimen of primitive christianity. "All of you, says he, in his epistle to Smyrna, follow after the Bishop, as Jesus Christ follows the Father.—Let no man without the Bishop do any of those things that ought to be done in the church.—Let that worship be accounted lawful, which is either performed by the Bishop himself, or permitted by him.—Whatsoever he approves is acceptable unto God." In his epistle to Polycarp.—" Attend to the Bishop as God doth to you, my soul for such as obey the Bishop, presbyters, and deacons, and with such let me have my portion in God." In his epistle to the Ephesians :—" Let us manifest that we ought to receive the Bishop as the Lord." To the Magnesians :—" Study to do all things in the concord of God, the Bishop presiding in the place of God, the presbyters in the place of the council of the Apostles, and my most sweet deacons having committed to them the service of Christ : — Therefore, as the Lord doth nothing without the Father, being one with him, so do ye nothing without the Bishop and the presbyters." In his epistle to the Philadelphians :—" As many as remain with the Bishop, these belong to God in Christ Jesus — I had this knowledge from no man, but the spirit preached, saying, without the Bishop see that ye do nothing." Once more, in his epistle to the Trallifians :—" Let all reverence the Deacons as the command of Christ Jesus, the Bishop as Jesus Christ, and the presbytery as the council of God and the senate of the Apostles, without which there is no church — I am not bound in any respect, but can be able to know things heavenly, the orders of Angels, their constitutions, principalities,

cipalities, things visible and invisible." Was ever such wild raving heard from a man in his sober senses?

I am sufficiently aware, at the same time, that these very passages, the effusions of a disordered brain as they may appear to those who take their religious creed entirely from the scriptures, have, by the patrons of the hierarchy, and the sticklers for sacerdotal power, been considered as an inestimable treasure, and quoted with mighty triumph. And, perhaps, it may be thought, by some of more moderate and rational principles, that so early a claim to superiority and direction, by a man so highly revered for sanctity, cannot fail to have some weight.

Before we proceed, therefore, we beg leave to offer the following considerations to the attention of the candid reader,—That, a man's having had an opportunity of knowing the mind of the Apostles, does not afford us sufficient evidence that he was, in fact, properly informed, did not labour under some mistake, or was not influenced by other motives than the knowledge and love of the truth. The Gospel was preached to all the churches in its most pure and simple state, in spirit and in power; by a divine commission, and with the promise of success: did they thefore obey the truth? did not a spirit of innovation and error, as we have had already occasion to observe, appear with unconquerable obstinacy, after every apostolic remonstrance and admonition? and are we to wonder if one man, amidst all his advantages of information, and reputed sanctity, should have been led into errors? The apostles had magnified *their* office;

are

are we to wonder, that, in such circumstances, the whole dignity and power which they claimed should be transferred to the succeeding order of ecclesiastics; where the office in general bore such a similarity? are we even to wonder, that religious enthusiasm mingling with the human passions should have led to a few unguarded expressions that seem to carry the point still higher than the apostles themselves had done? If you are to search for the time when religious fervours, and a heated imagination are likeliest to operate upon the mind, and hurry men away before their understandings are sufficiently informed, and their views corrected by different observations, you will find it in the violence of first impressions, and the succeeding ferments of a newly awakened zeal. The mind, in such circumstances, is raised above its native tone, and scorns the cool boundaries of reason and moderation. Neither, therefore, the supposed sanctity, nor the antiquity of this father's testimony are, of themselves, sufficient to render his authority valid.

But in every question of this kind, there is one of two things necessary, I apprehend, to satisfy every fair inquirer:—That a writer's-testimony is properly supported by the Scriptures;—or, that it carry the marks of credibility in itself. With respect to the *first*, it will no doubt be urged, in the present case; that, however arrogant these expressions may appear to be, or however assuming the sacerdotal claim implied in them, they are sufficiently justified by the words of our Lord himself:—" He that heareth you heareth me, and he that despiseth you despiseth me." Now if these words, which it is acknowledged, exprefs a very high authority, be, indeed, a good plea for the venerable father, or hath any argument in it for the pretenfions of priefts, why ftop fhort without taking in the whole extent of the commiffion? " Behold I give unto you power to tread on serpents and fcorpions, and over all the power of the enemy, and nothing fhall by any means hurt you." This is certainly comprehended in the original commiffion: why then not include both parts of it as they ftand connected together, and ferve to explain one another? But as this would exceed the higheft prerogative that Ecclefiaftics have affumed, it may be thought more modeft to plead on the laft commiffion given to Apoftles, and which, it may be faid, defcends in all its force, and extent, to every minifter of religion to the end of the world — or, at leaft, to Bifhops, the fucceffors of the Apoftles, agreeably to the plain words of it, " Lo I am with you even to the end of the world." And again, " The glory which thou gaveft me, I have given them, that they may be one, as we are one." To fhow the fallacy of every argument of this kind deduced from thefe, or any fimilar texts of Scripture, it is only neceffary here to obferve, *firft*, that it is evident, from fact, that this commiffion to the Apoftles did not defcend in all its force, and extent, to any fucceeding Ecclefiaftic, or order of Ecclefiaftics, even in the age immediately fucceeding the Apoftles: and it will be allowed, on all hands, that, fo far as it regards vifible and extraordinary powers, the efficacy of it hath ceafed for upwards, at leaft, of fourteen centuries, without one pretence of performing works above the ordinary ftandard of humanity, where ignorance and fuperftition had not

afforded

afforded an easy opportunity for every *priestly* delusion: so that this commission, if it respects modern Ecclesiastics, is indisputably limited in the order of Providence; and how far this limitation extends, and what powers are derived from it, is the only question — a question which we shall have occasion to discuss in the sequel at large. *Secondly,* the glory which Christ gave his Apostles was neither the same in kind, in *every* respect, nor in degree, in *any*, with what he had received from the Father; not can it be pretended, from what hath been observed, that it was the same, in *either* view, that the Apostles gave to the succeeding ministers of religion: so that all such Scriptural authorities are utterly vague and indefinite with regard to the transmission of Ecclesiastic powers.—They either justify the claim to every Apostolic power, or to none.

But what have the Scriptures to do in this matter? The good father doth not so much as claim this authority: he soars higher, " He had knowledge of it from *no man*, but the *spirit* preached, saying, without the Bishop see that ye do nothing." Now do not imagine, reader, that this preaching is the preaching of the Apostolic word, or information in any shape communicated by the Apostles, which, in a general sense, may be called the preaching of the spirit. By no means; for the Apostles were men, and spoke and acted as men, however aided by the spirit; but *he* had the knowledge of it from *no man*. He had it, therefore, by immediate revelation from God, which rendered every other standard not only unnecessary, but made discoveries to him of which the Scriptures give no account. " I am not bound in any respect, but can be able to know things heavenly, the order of Angels, their constitutions, principalities, things visible and invisible." Who, after so modest a testimony in his own favour, would be bold enough to call in question the authority of this champion for the hierarchy?

THE *second* thing necessary to support the credit of a writer is, that what he asserts carries the marks of credibility in itself — if it is a fact, that it is not improbable — if it is a doctrine, that it is not repugnant to our ideas of God, as the moral and righteous governor of the world; or to the nature of man, as a moral and accountable agent. Now, the question before us is, whether it be consistent with those ideas, to suppose any denomination of men on earth, whether bishop, presbyter, or deacon, vested with those unlimited powers, which this writer would ascribe to those characters? It is here supposed, that the *Bishop* is to the *flock*, over which he presides, what the *Father* is to the *Son*, which, without supposing the Bishop possessed of infallible and uncontroulable powers, is perfectly absurd. Now to suppose a Bishop, as such, vested with unlimited and uncontroulable powers, and without which the argument can be of no avail to Ecclesiastics; — that is to account every act of worship lawful which he performs, and to believe that whatever he approves is acceptable unto God: — is an unlimited confidence which no man owes to another, and is utterly inconsistent with our rational and moral powers; and, therefore, utterly inconsistent with every idea of that wise and moral Being who hath endowed us with them. — The Apostle Paul himself claimed

CHAP. II.   OF TRADITION.   53

claimed no more, than that the churches should be followers of him, as he was of Jesus Christ;—not as Jesus Christ was of the Father. They claimed obedience *in the Lord*, that is, agreeably to the evidence they exhibited of their divine commission, and the instructions they had delivered to the different societies of christians by authority from their Lord; and therefore cannot be supposed, as shall be more fully explained afterwards, to have given unlimited and unconditional powers to any man, or number of men, to propose new articles of faith, or new rules of obedience to christians in any future period.

But, however men may be led through ignorance, enthusiasm, prejudices, or party views, to pervert doctrines, it may be thought, that practices or institutes are by no means exposed to the same danger, and, therefore, that traditions relative to these might with safety have been committed to the primitive societies of christians, and with unlimited confidence, and absolute security, received from them.—We have a direct proof of the contrary, and how far a superstitious credulity prevailed, in the grand controversy concerning the celebration of Easter; an early controversy that divided the eastern and western churches:—Polycarp, in the one, alledging the authority of John, whose disciple he had been:—Anicetus, in the other, that of Peter and Paul. "Here, says a judicious writer, it is most remarkable, how, even, in the most early times they heaped falsehood upon falsehood, and supported one forgery with another. The fable of Peter's being at Rome, and of conjuring Simon Magus there, was even then begun to obtain;

D 3   whereof

whereof the Romanists made their advantage, and began to ascribe to him some headship over the rest; and then averred, that he had appointed them, not only to celebrate Easter, but also had enjoined them to keep it on the *fifteenth*, and not on the *fourteenth* day of the month, as did the eastern churches. Now that they, in their turn, might be even with the Romanists, and meet them after their own fashion and arts, the Asians invented the like legends of the Apostle John, who, as they alledged, died at Ephesus, and enjoined them to keep Easter on the *fourteenth* day, but *by no means* on the *fifteenth:* and the better to set off the fable, Polycarpus of Ephesus, in his letter to Victor, harangues the praises of John, that thereby they may be induced to prefer him to Peter; and sticks not to assert, that John was a priest, and wore a high priest's golden crown: and yet, it is acknowledged, that John was not of the priestly race, and far less was the high priest, to whom, of all the priests such a crown was peculiar."—Now here it is to be observed, that the probability is, that there were not any such injunctions left to one or other of the churches concerning the celebration of Easter. It is an institution no where mentioned in the New Testament. The word is not to be found, but in one place, " Intending after Easter to bring him forth to the people," and where, it is evident, that the plain English ought to have been, after the passover.—But supposing the fact, that certain injunctions and directions had been given by one, or more Apostles, concerning the time, manner, and obligation of observing this institution; we evidently see, from this early and violent opposition, that it is impossible to arrive at any certainty, where

the

the written record doth not furnish a plain and unerring standard.—The chief leaders in religion had so early run wild after their own fancies, or were led to deviate from the Scriptures to support some political views, or some favourite system of their own; that neither doctrines not institutions could have been safe in their hands.—While christianity was yet in its infancy, the *enemy* had begun to scatter tares among the wheat; and thus, gradually, to collect materials for rearing up the monstrous fabrick of the *mystery of iniquity:* so that, if the sacred writings, by the signal interposition and superintendency of Providence, had not been preserved so genuine and unadulterated, that their authenticity is admitted on all hands, it would have been impossible to have known what to have admitted, or what to have rejected; what had been originally the revelation of God, or what, under that sacred authority, through weakness had been adopted, or by policy had been imposed upon mankind.

In illustration and support of this argument, we may, with propriety, observe here, that the same pretensions to traditions, and the same abuse of them appeared in the Jewish church.—The Jews were possessed of the only written inspired law; a law given with the utmost solemnity, and held in the most profound veneration; a law which descended to the most minute circumstances of worship, and sufficiently definitive with regard to moral and political duties; a law which they were at liberty, neither to add to, nor diminish from: " The book of the law shall not depart from thy mouth, but thou shalt meditate thereon day and night;—ye shall not add to the word of this commandment, neither shall ye diminish from it." But could this people be restrained from their own inventions and superadditions, even by an inhibition so plain and absolute? They could not. There were *fathers* in the Jewish, as well as the Christian church: good men no doubt, and who were supposed to carry authority in all their decisions; but unhappily credulous in adopting, or ingenious in contriving new tenets, and possessed of a truly *priestly* zeal in laying burdens on the consciences of men, sometimes as an addition, sometimes in direct opposition to the written law. The traditional reveries of the *elders* were held, not only of equal importance with it, but had, in many instances, corrupted, and, in some, superseded it altogether. Of this Christ Jesus repeatedly complains, and charges them expressly with having made the word of God of none effect by their traditions.

This observation leads us to two things equally plain and conclusive in this argument:—It confirms the account that hath been given of the mischievous tendency of traditionary pretences, in corrupting the purity both of doctrine and worship; and that, whatever we may suppose traditions to be in their original form, it seems impossible, in the ordinary course of things, to preserve them from degenerating into fable and absurdity, or being employed by designing men for their own ambitious purposes.—It shows, by itself, and exclusive of every other argument, the absurdity of imagining, that the Saviour of the world, or any of those immediately authorised by him, in the immediate view of such pretentions,

tentions, and such abuse founded on tradition, whether supposed or real, should have exposed his perfect law to the same danger; should have committed orally any doctrines, precepts, or institutes of his religion to any man, or number of men, to be handled by them at discretion. Whoever will bestow but half a thought in comparing the Old and New Dispensations, will immediately perceive, that the last is much more liable to abuse than the first; it being far easier to preserve by tradition an external mode of worship, consisting of certain rites and performances peculiar to itself, and which soon becomes familiar, is confirmed by habit, and naturally acquires a superstitious veneration; than to preserve doctrines, and a spiritual worship, wholly intended to cultivate an inward temper of virtue and devotion.—And if infinite wisdom, even with regard to that dispensation, saw it not fit to trust any thing to tradition, to suppose that this ground of evidence is admissible in the christian system, would appear, on all the principles of analogy, utterly inconsistent.

SECT. VI.

Of the Scriptures as a perfect Rule of Faith.

HAVING proved, it is presumed, on all the principles of reason, experience, and analogy, that tradition is not to be admitted as a proper source of information, or an authentic ground of credibility: it remains, that we endeavour to prove, that the Scriptures are a perfect and compleat rule of faith, independent of every supplemental aid.

It hath already been shown, that to suppose the sacred penmen committed one part to writing, and another to tradition; both stamped with the same divine authority;—would be perfectly absurd. Let us now appeal to the Sacred Record itself.

At the time of our Lord's appearance, the divine law had, in a great measure, lost its authority, and the people had become the mere dupes of legendary tales. The prophets, it seems, had early discovered the prelude to this abuse — a licentious spirit in wandering after lying *priests*; and, therefore, as the only effectual cure, reminded them of the perfection of the divine law, and referred them to it, " Should not a people seek to their God?" True; but might they not seek to their God by consulting every source of information;—and might there not be other means besides the written laws? No; " To the law and the testimony, if they speak not according to this word, it is because there is no light in them." They, who? "-Familiar spirits and wizards that peep and mutter." Now whether these familiar spirits spoke by false prophets, or elders, uttering lies in the name of the Lord, and pretending to things not authorised by the written record, made no difference: every truth necessary for them to know was contained in the law, and an appeal to every other standard is precluded.

Our Lord confirms the same doctrine. For a discovery of his true character, and the nature of his mission, he appeals to the Old Testament, which, if consulted with candour and attention, he declares sufficient to remove

move every prejudice the Jews entertained against him. "Search the Scriptures,—for they are they which testify of me;" again, when the rich man is represented as humbly supplicating Father Abraham to send a messenger from the other world to warn and admonish his brethren;—the answer is a remarkable and decisive evidence in what view the antient law was to be considered: "If they will not hear Moses and the Prophets, neither would they be persuaded, should one arise from the dead." The law of Moses, and the Prophets explaining, and inculcating that law, was alone sufficient for the attainment of that happiness, and avoiding of that misery which the rich man had in his eye, till God should see fit to impart some additional discovery of his will.— Now, if the law given to Moses, if the instructions and admonitions of the Prophets committed to writing, and preserved by the Jewish Church, were thus perfect for all the purposes for which that dispensation was intended; can we reasonably suppose, that the grace and truth which came by Jesus Christ, and which comprehended the moral part of the former;—that this dispensation which included the last discovery of God to man, is less perfect as a rule of faith? Can we possibly allow ourselves to think, that every thing oral was excluded from the former, and that the perfection of the latter should depend on a multiplicity of unwritten traditions? Nothing could be more absurd. From the perfection of the one, therefore, we have the strongest presumptive proof of the perfection of the other.

But independently of every presumptive proof, we have a variety of intrinsic ones from the dispensation itself felf. As every section in this chapter hath an immediate tendency to corroborate the point in view, I confine myself to one. "All scripture is given by the inspiration of God, and is useful for doctrine, for reproof, for instruction in righteousness, that the man of God may be perfect, furnished unto good works." It may, perhaps, be said that by scripture *here* is meant the writings of the Old Testament: and I do not pretend to say they are excluded, or that by scripture, in the apostolic writings, is not generally understood the old dispensation: but that the words must have a particular reference to the peculiar doctrines of christianity recorded in the new, which were now generally committed to writing, and in the hands of the different christian societies, can admit of no doubt — this being one of the last, if not the last of St. Paul's epistles. But whether we consider the words as including both dispensations, so far as regards the moral and spiritual part, and as the first serves to prove and illustrate the last; or whether as respecting the christian only, the argument is the same: It is of scripture the apostle speaks, some thing written in which Timothy was taught, and which, exclusive of every other source of information, was able to make him wise unto salvation. This will appear more fully from a short review and explication of the words — "Profitable for doctrine," for a discovery of our duty; for what is doctrine but something taught that was not known before, or something formerly taught enforced from new arguments and motives? "so that by profitable for doctrine", the apostle evidently means, that the great excellency of the written word is, that herein we are instructed in every doctrine necessary for us to be made acquainted with for attaining

eternal

eternal happiness—" For reproof, for correction,"—for discovering errors either in faith or practice, removing prejudices, bringing us to a sense of duty when we have erred, and in every matter of dispute holding up a perfect and infallible rule; for awakening obstinate and presumptuous sinners, and carrying home conviction with force and propriety. " For instruction in righteousness;" what those duties are which we owe to one another, wherein that holiness consists which is the foundation of true happiness, and by what means it is to be carried forward, and perfected in the soul.—These are the great things for which the written record is profitable, according to the Apostle; and, to every attentive reader of the New Testament, it must appear plain, that this is the summary of it; and that the great design of the sacred writers is, to unfold, and enforce these several points at large.

If it should be objected, that, though these are things highly profitable — even necessary, it doth not from thence follow, that nothing farther is necessary: because, what is necessary to a subject, is not, therefore, supposed to contain all the constituent parts of it. And so far it must be allowed, that a thing may be essential to a subject, that doth not constitute the whole of it— in other words, that we can suppose a written record, and tradition, necessary in their several degrees to perfect an evidence. But this distinction cannot take place here. The Apostle expresly precludes it, by explaining immediately what he means by profitable.—That the Scriptures of the inspiration of God, are profitable, not merely by comparison with other things which are unprofitable,

profitable, or less profitable; but that they alone are profitable, so as to answer the several purposes he enumerates; and which put together, furnish the man of God unto good works;—make him wise unto salvation, and render him perfect. Now, what furnishes every thing necessary for accomplishing an end, is perfect with regard to that end, and excludes every thing else. What renders the man of God perfect is a perfect rule, and requires no addition.

SECT. VII.

EXCEPTIONS AGAINST THE REASONING IN THE FOREGOING SECTIONS REMOVED.

TO invalidate the force of the reasoning against tradition in the foregoing pages, three things may be urged —That natural religion, or the first discoveries of God to man, were transmitted through this channel to succeeding ages —That the purity of the Scriptures themselves must have wholly depended on the fidelity of the *Church*, and if she deserve credit with regard to the Scriptures, why not with regard to tradition? If she hath been accounted a faithful repository in the one case, why not in the other? — That the Scriptures themselves plainly refer to Apostolic traditions, as a rule of faith.

It doth not appear to me, that any thing else having the colour of argument can be offered. These therefore, we shall examine into, and be able, it is hoped, to show, that, however seemingly plausible, they have no weight in them.

First,

First, with regard to natural religion, let it be observed, that it did not consist, as is here supposed, in directions and precepts delivered to our common parent—The knowledge of God, and his duty arose from the faculties by which his nature was distinguished; that is, the original impressions stamped on his mind by the hand of the Creator, along with the conclusions he was fitted, by the exercise of his reason, to draw from the works of nature, his own frame, and the œconomy of Providence around him. Of any other discovery, at least, we know nothing to the calling of Abraham, the original promise, and the prohibition to Noah excepted, and what may, in general be gathered from the external rite of sacrificing; which, being deducible from no known principle in the human mind, seems to have drawn its origin from revelation. And so long as mankind were disposed to pay attention to these sacred impressions, to the dictates of sound reason, and this benevolent, and wise order of nature, nothing further seems to have been necessary—Without, indeed, supposing reason and conscience, characteristic faculties of our natures, every revelation would have been in vain; and to suppose these original and distinguishing faculties without any impressions of a Divinity, or any capacity of tracing the Creator in his works, any sense of dependence or moral obligation seems perfectly absurd. — It may be asked for what end were they given? To form a capability of feeling the obligation of moral duties, will it be said, and of reasoning from those ideas, with which his mind would be furnished by an after revelation? This is, at best, but an idle round about, and, which is more, supposes that a moral and reasonable being was made by the

the constitution of his nature incapable of feeling or reasoning. For if he was capable of either, what was more natural, what was of more importance to him, as an immediate object, than God and his duty?

ADMITTING, however, at present, that our ideas of God and our duty were originally derived from revelation alone, and transmitted by tradition. It is sufficient to observe *here*—That the prodigious duration of human life previous to the flood, between which, and the creation, there were scarcely two generations, must have proved the most probable means of preserving oral doctrines, supposing any such to have been given during that period—That, even in this period, and notwithstanding all the advantages of transmission by which it was distinguished, the knowledge of God and a sense of duty, a few instances excepted, were almost extinguished amidst universal idolatry and impiety—That after the flood, whatever traditionary information might have been transmitted from Noah or his sons, an universal ignorance and corruption of manners soon followed—" The knowledge of God, and the memory of the creation began to decay gradually, and the fables which succeeded the ancient tradition retained but gross ideas of them." This gave occasion to the calling of Abraham, in less than five hundred years from the deluge; in whose family a sense of religion was preserved, not by tradition merely, but by various and signal manifestations, and interpositions of Providence. The argument, therefore, from the topic of natural religion lies the other way, and concludes, not in favour of tradition, but for the necessity of a written law.

THE

The *second* exception is, that the authenticity of the written record rests entirely upon the same authority with tradition — the fidelity of those who have transmitted both; that it is, therefore, unreasonable to receive the one, and to reject the other. This is the sum of an argument, artfully coloured over, and speciously declaimed upon, — and which your traditionary men exhibit on all occasions with an air of decision to their implicit votaries. But a few sentences will satisfy the impartial and attentive reader that it is mere sophistry. For *first*, this sort of reasoning in favour of tradition, if it proves any thing, proves too much: it sets aside the use of writing altogether, so that there never had been occasion for any book to this day; because every book must have depended on the fidelity of those through whose hands it hath passed down from age to age, and every book that shall be written must depend on the fidelity of succeeding ages; now if those who have been the instruments of transmitting a book for seventeen hundred years past, or shall be the instruments of transmitting one for seventeen hundred years to come, if the world shall last so long, should have been, or are to be considered as equally fit for transmitting the contents of it by tradition, as the book itself; it may be affirmed, that there never was any occasion at all for writing a book, if the subject of it were fairly made known, and never will to the end of the world. — But *secondly*, the fact is, that there is an immense difference between preserving the contents of a written record pure, and transmitting traditions with any degree of credibility, could their origin be ascertained, which is impossible;—a difference so obvious, that the very men who may be disposed to propagate the fictions of fancy, or the dreams of a disordered mind; the spectres of superstition, or the delusions of enthusiasm; the wonders of credulity, or the more artful inventions of *priestcraft*, may not have it in their power to adulterate a written record: it being extremely difficult to introduce any material alterations into a book, without a discovery, after it hath passed through many hands, and been generally read and known. And, with regard to the book in question, there are peculiar circumstances, that would have rendered any design of this kind morally impossible.—A book held so sacred so generally spread, so frequently and publicly read, appealed to on so many different occasions, opposed by enemies, defended by friends, translated into different languages, and almost transcribed into different authors; these and many more circumstances, afford all the evidence the subject is capable of, that no material alteration could have been introduced into the sacred record: an evidence infinitely superior to any thing that can possibly be alledged in favour of tradition, where there is no public, original, authenticated standard to which, in case of doubt or opposition, we can have recourse.

WILL it be asked, by way of objection,— do the epistles then, contain all that the inspired writers taught? Are all the transactions of the first ministers of religion, so numerous, and who laboured so abundantly, confined to the narrow limits of a little volume? No indeed; no more than all that our Lord said and did is narrated by the four Evangelists. The latter informs us of every thing necessary for us to know during his abode on earth; and the former, of every thing left

in

in commission to his Apostles, now that he is gone to heaven, till he come again.—The Apostolic manner of instruction and address, and the several topics insisted upon, would, no doubt, be different according to the temper, prejudices, degrees of knowledge, and peculiar circumstances of the churches; a sample of which almost every epistle furnishes: but they had but *one* gospel to preach, in its leading and capital doctrines the same to all. From this variety, great indulgencies, in particular cases, to the prepossessions of its new converts might be necessary; hence different practices, and different external forms, would prevail; not owing to any positive law, or, even, to the genius of Christianity, but merely to that prudence and wisdom which are always disposed to yield in lesser, and in themselves indifferent things, to obtain greater: of this prudence the Apostle Paul was himself a striking example; and he seems to have established it as a rule among the churches. — But because Paul purified himself according to the law, took a vow and shaved his head, that he might not give offence to the zealous Jews, will it therefore follow, that this ought to be a standing ordinance in the church of Christ? Or, because certain Christian Societies might have been indulged by the Apostles, or first ministers of religion in similar practices in condescension to certain prejudices, which it would have been imprudent to oppose; is their example to be established into a model carrying the authority of law in it? Nothing could be more absurd.

But are not traditions referred to by the apostle Paul himself? " Therefore brethren, stand fast, and hold the traditions which ye have been taught whether by word or epiftle." That the Apoftle fpeaks here of traditions is not difputed, but what thefe traditions were becomes the queftion — whether traditions exclufive of the written word, and intended as a fupplement to it bearing the force of a law to all the churches of Chrift to the end of the world? — Whether peculiar to the particular fituation of thofe to whom he writes? — Or, whether certain points that had been preached to the churches, but not yet committed to writing? The laft evidently appears to have been the cafe. The canon of Scripture was not only not compleated at this time, but this was among the firft epiftles written to the churches; and, therefore, the Apoftle may well be fuppofed to refer to feveral things not particularly mentioned in his epiftles to the Theffalonians; what had been delivered orally to them, or to the other churches, but afterwards committed to writing, would juftly be confidered as traditions, till the whole epiftles were collected, and every particular Chriftian Society had opportunity to examine and compare the whole facred code: for it will not be faid, that every particular epiftle contains the whole doctrines aud precepts of Chriftianity. — Or, we may fuppofe, with great propriety, that particular directions were orally delivered by the Apoftles, relative to the extraordinary circumftances of the churches at that time, which it was, by no means, neceffary to commit to writing, as being of little confequence to the ordinary, and fettled ftate of Chriftianity:—What could not take place in any other fituation, or, but in one fimilar, could not be defigned as a permanent and unalterable directory.—Something analagous to this, is always the

cafe

case in every infant society. In one or other of these views, the words admit of a plain and sensible interpretation, without supposing that the Apostle intended to establish a system of traditions as an additional rule of faith: traditions of which we know nothing, and which, therefore, under this general denomination, might be rendered subservient, at pleasure, to the purposes of those who had presumption enough to impose them upon the weak and credulous.—It were just as much to the purpose to tell us what the parchments contained which the same Apostle left at Troas. From this sacred roll, for ought I know, a new gospel might have been made out. The authority of the *Church* was equally good for both, seeing we are equally ignorant of either: for it only required boldness enough to maintain, that they were found at such a time, and in such a place, and contained such doctrines and institutions, as one was pleased to authenticate; and the whole matter was at an end. For, if once we are brought to resolve our faith into an implicit assent to any tribunal upon earth, sense or nonsense, truth or falsehood, possibility or impossibility, are admitted with equal ease.

CHAP. III.

OF THE RIGHTS OF CONSCIENCE AND PRIVATE JUDGMENT.

SECT I.

OF THE REASONS OF THIS INQUIRY.

THE ground we have gained in the preceding pages, in expofing the weaknefs and abfurdity of all traditionary pretences, and eftablifhing the Scriptures as a perfect rule of faith, is of no importance at all, if it ftill remain a queftion — Whether individuals have a right of inquiry, and judging for themfelves; or whether any man, or number of men upon earth, the *Church*, a general council, or the fupreme Pontiff dictating from his chair, are vefted with the exclufive privilege of interpreting the facred record, and determining finally in all religious controverfies; it precifely amounting to the fame thing in this cafe, whether you hold or reject traditions, how many, or of what kind thefe traditions are. If I am not at liberty to ufe my own underftanding, he, or they who have affumed the leading of it, and to whom I believe in confcience, I am bound to fubmit, may make Scripture tradition, or tradition Scripture.

It will be of importance, therefore, if we can throw fome light upon this queftion: a queftion however interefting teresting to protestants, as the bulwark of those civil and religious rights which they profess to hold most sacred, and, however fully explained, and warmly defended in opposition to the claim of the church of Rome, which, nevertheless, they seem wholly to forget in their reasonings, and conduct to one another: so that while they acknowledge, in words, that the Scriptures are the rule of faith, and alone sufficient to make men wise unto Salvation, and every party is well disposed to judge for themselves; they appear extremely jealous of granting the same liberty to one another; and, instead of the Scriptures, would slip in their own explications and comments, bind their decisions upon others an infallible standard, and oblige them to see with *their* eyes.— And what is this but popery under another name? It is the worst, and most pernicious part of it. For of what importance is it to society, whether I believe in transubstantiation or not, whether I fall down before an image, or pray to a Saint or not. If I err, I err alone: but he who claims a right over my understanding, and pretends to establish a creed to which I must declare my assent under certain pains and penalties, injurious to my rights as a good member of the commmonwealth, attacks the common privileges of society. From the same principles he would be led to enslave mankind altogether; however at present he may intend no such thing, however he may dissemble his purposes, or, however he may not have in his power a proper opportunity of executing them.

It is intended, however, in treating of this subject, to take a more extensive view of it, and to inquire how far the rights of conscience, and private judgment, are affected, *first*, by the laws of political government — and, *secondly*, by the laws of christianity; that is, as members of civil and christian society.

SECT. II.

OF THE INFLUENCE OF SOCIETY UPON THE RIGHTS OF CONSCIENCE AND PRIVATE JUDGMENT.

IN attending to man as a social being, or a member of civil society, we must not overlook the higher relation he stands in as a moral agent; because this is characteristic of his nature. It is the primary law by which the great Creator intended to direct our conduct, and is the foundation of every other duty; and from which, therefore, we cannot possibly be absolved by any human authority. It is in its own nature unalienable and incapable of being transferred. It is universal, immutable, eternal. Now it is conscience that feels the force of this law, and the obligations we lie under to comply with it — or in other words conscience, which properly constitutes a moral and accountable agent, is the distinguishing law of our natures. As beings, therefore, immediately under this law, every individual is obliged to conform himself to his own ideas of right and wrong; that is to those intimations of duty and those obligations which arise from his state of dependence, the blessings he enjoys, and the future hopes he entertains. — Indeed nothing could be more absurd than to suppose, that the all-wise, all-gracious Author of our beings should have constituted our natures so, as to make our happiness, or our misery to result from the approbation, or disapprobation of our own minds, and yet

yet that it should become our duty, not to judge for ourselves where conscience alone was concerned. This would be to counteract the very design of understanding and conscience, and to supersede, at once, the great law of our creation.

Hence it appears, that the relation in which we stand to society cannot possibly encroach upon those rights that belong to us as moral beings; because a prior or superior obligation cannot possibly be weakened, much less set aside, by that which is evidently subsequent and inferior — And yet, it cannot be denied that *this* relation doth oblige us to certain concessions, and to submit to certain laws and conditions founded merely on human authority, to which antecedently, and considered as individuals, we were not bound.

As it is of importance to mark with some precision, how far these obligations extend, I beg leave just to mention those cases, where, from the nature, and by the fundamental laws of all civilized societies, individuals can transfer their rights to others, and are bound to conform themselves to measures established by lawful authority, and not to their own ideas of right and wrong.

And, in general, the great end of all civil society being to procure, and maintain such temporal articles and outward advantages, as in a separate and single state would be impossible; it is obvious that for this end certain general laws are necessary. Now, as laws cannot be made, all at once, so as to be adapted to every possible case; as they must receive additions, improvements, and alterations according to the growth, and different

different circumstances of society; some person, or persons, must be entrusted with this power, as the various exigences of the state may require; that is — there must be a LEGISLATIVE power. But as laws are of no avail, but as they are properly enforced and rendered effectual, the right of executing the laws, and judging finally in all questions where individuals cannot agree, must be lodged in hands different from the legislative; that is there must be an EXECUTIVE power. Both these powers must necessarily take place in every well regulated society; because they are equally necessary for the common security. This being observed it follows;

First, that government ought to be considered as a part of the divine constitution for promoting the happiness of mankind—That as the all-wise Creator hath formed us with natures that lead us to society, and with wants that cannot be supplied but in a social state, whatever regulations, laws, ordinances, offices, are necessary, and most subservient for promoting this end, are approved of, and authorised by him; and consequently that obedience to the higher powers, and fulfilling the engagements, that either formally, or virtually arise from the different stations we hold, is a moral duty — where such obedience, and such engagements do not obviously contradict that higher allegiance, which we antecedently owe to the great Lord of the world, which no subsequent relation can possibly vacate or dissolve.

Secondly, that whatever advantages we enjoy as members of any particular society, may be defined and limited by that society, or those to whom the powers of
legislation

legiſlation are committed; and the minority are not only bound to ſubmit, but to co-operate with the general laws: or, if individuals will refuſe to acquieſce, much more if they will reſiſt and oppoſe, they are to be conſidered as enemies to, and counteracting the fundamental laws of ſociety.—If I purchaſe an eſtate or landed property for a juſt equivalent, it becomes my own perſonal right, and he who would attempt to ſeize any part of it by fraud or violence, would be guilty of a manifeſt injury, and be amenable to the laws of the ſociety of which I am a member; but though this eſtate is my own perſonal property, it is a property thus rendered ſecure by the *ſame* laws; as this ſecurity, therefore, is of real value, and as a public aſſeſſment or tax may be neceſſary for the ſupport and preſervation of the common intereſt, I am undoubtedly bound to contribute the rate or proportion of ſuch tax or aſſeſſment as ſhall be laid upon it by truſtees appointed by the public for that end—Acting on the ſame principles, ſhould a diſpute happen concerning property, or any emolument I had laid claim to as a member of the ſociety, I am bound to ſubmit to the deciſion of judges eſtabliſhed by the general laws, and veſted with the ſole juriſdiction of deciding finally in queſtions of this nature: I may think myſelf injured, perhaps I am ſo, but the object of diſpute being plainly cognizable by the public, and determined in the laſt reſort, agreeably to the common forms, it becomes my duty quietly to ſubmit, and hold the deciſion a legal and valid one, for the ſame reaſons that I ſhould approve of, or judge any reference neceſſary at all: for all ſuch caſes ought to be conſidered as of the nature of a reference or

ſubmiſſion

submission for terminating differences about which individuals would never agree.

Thirdly, with regard to measures planned and carried forward for the public weal, it ought further to be admitted, that individuals are not at liberty to act on the principles of private judgment, or to regulate their conduct by their own ideas of fitness and unfitness; because, in this case, it is self-evident, that universal anarchy would ensue, and all government be at an end; which would necessarily issue in one of two things:—That fraud and violence would prevail, till the stronger party should enslave the weaker;—Or, that reverting by joint consent to the security of common laws, individuals would be brought to see the necessity of acting, not according to their own ideas, but the decisions of the public; so that, in the nature of things, common laws, and measures enacted by legal authority, are supposed to preclude the right of private judgment.

Fourthly, that in every well constituted society there must be certain stations, where inferiors are obliged to execute the sentences of superiors in contradiction to their own opinions; because without such implicit obedience, the several departments of government would not be carried forward, nor the laws rendered effectual. Nothing could be more absurd, than a scheme of government, where the lowest officer in the state was left to judge for himself, and to plead his own convictions in opposition to the indispensable duties of his station. His conduct, in this case, hath no concern with the rule of his private judgment; implicit obedience is the supposed,

posed, and necessary condition on which he holds his office, and, while he continues in it, his obligation is absolute.—In all these cases private judgment is bound to submit to the public:—and, in general, while things remain in a doubtful state, and measures appear in one light to one, and in another light to another, and these measures merely regard the political advantages we hold as members of civil society, the subject is not absolved from obedience, and inconsistently offers the plea of conscience. Or, if he should call in religion in support of his opposition, or disobedience, he may, perhaps, act consistently with regard to his own ideas of right and wrong, but he evidently betrays his want of understanding; and the execution of the laws neither can, nor ought to pay any regard to his scruples. The public order and safety is the grand object in the eye of the law, which cannot possibly admit of condescensions to individuals, which would necessarily imply a toleration utterly inconsistent with the foundations of government. But if, ceasing to be doubtful, public measures should appear to the majority, manifestly inconsistent with the essential laws of the constitution, and a direct violation of the common rights of society; the grand design of government being hereby overturned, the society is thrown upon its original ground, and called upon to act for its own safety.

SECT.

SECT. III.

OF THE INFLUENCE OF CHRISTIANITY ON THE RIGHTS OF CONSCIENCE AND PRIVATE JUDGMENT.

HAVING drawn a few outlines sufficient to mark the authority and extent of civil prerogative, and how far submission is due consistently with the rights of conscience and private judgment, upon the principles of natural religion; it is now proper to inquire, if, by the laws of Christianity, these distinguishing faculties of our nature are laid under any further restraints.

And, in order to illustrate this question, it may be in the general observed, that no revelation from God can possibly contradict those original feelings that are characteristic of our natures; because this would destroy every test by which we could possibly judge of truth or falsehood, virtue or vice: for what test or rule of action could be established more authentic, or more sacred? Or, if it could, by what evidence are you to judge of it? There must be some standard within yourself, call it by what name you please, to which, upon the whole, you must have recourse, and by which you are enabled to judge of ultimate, or mediate, fitness and propriety. Without this you are incapable of directing your own conduct, or receiving direction from any other quarter. However, therefore, it may be true, that the mind of man, without any further discovery from God, is unable to furnish a compleat rule of duty, or to lead us to the

whole

whole extent of that happiness of which our natures are capable; it may be affirmed, without exalting the human powers above what they really are, that they are still possessed of a capacity of judging, by an appeal to our own minds, whether a revelation pretended to be from God be worthy of him, and carry marks of credebility in it, with regard both to its internal and external evidence.—One may be sufficiently conscious of his own ignorance, and see the necessity of some additional discovery, and yet be able with some certainty, from the ideas of moral fitness and probability, of which he is still possessed, to say whether he be greatly misled or not, if such a discovery shall be made to him.—In the same manner that a traveller, who may be incapable of directing his own way without a guide, may yet remember so many standing conspicuous marks, as to pronounce, with some assurance, that his guide doth not impose upon him. Now, as understanding and conscience, so far as these do not exceed their proper limits, by presuming to encroach upon the fundamental laws of society, are undoubtedly the rule of our conduct, as rational and moral beings; (see p. 92, 93 of this section) it appears that a revelation from God cannot destroy the privileges included in these leading faculties of our natures; and consequently that all the arguments which tyrants and *priests* would deduce from the Scriptures, to subject these higher powers in matters wholly moral, to human authority, can serve only, in proportion as they appear conclusive, to beget suspicions against Christianity as unfriendly to human nature; and, instead of proving a valuable acquisition to our knowledge and improvement—to render our state infinitely more wretched.

This reasoning, it may be thought by some, is intended to furnish a pretence for rejecting any evidence, that may be supposed to be derived from this quarter, against the claim which we would here explain and vindicate. Far otherwise—we are certain no such evidence can be produced; nor are we afraid of any attempt this way—on the contrary, we shall make it appear that, while the New Testament confirms the account we have given of those obligations we owe as members of *civil* society, it leaves the rights of conscience and private judgment entire, as members of christian society—The former reasoning, therefore, hath been chiefly introduced to show, that christianity supports and fortifies this claim, and thereby receives additional lustre, and confirmation of its divinity.

For, in the *first* place, it considers the king as supreme, and governors, in general, as the *ordinance of man*; and yet the powers that be as *ordained of God:* that is, government, as respecting its external form, depending on variable causes—times, circumstances, and the genius of a people; but under some form or other, necessary for the order and happiness of society and, therefore, divine or immediately authorised of God, and binding on the subject in point of conscience, so far as regards the publick utility and welfare—but not extending further, or subjecting the conscience, in general, to the decisions of any human tribunal; " Be subject not only for wrath, but also for conscience sake; for this cause ye pay tribute also." Where, it is evident, that, with regard to such things only as are included in the idea of civil government, the Apostle extends the obligations

obligations of conscience. The command of the civil magistrate is of no force when it exceeds these bounds; "Did not we strictly command you that ye should not "preach in this name? And Peter and the other Apostles answered and said, we ought to obey God rather than man."

But the sense of the sacred writers, on this part of our subject, may be collected into one point of view from a single passage — the decision of our Lord himself in this very case: "Render unto Cæsar the things that are Cæsar's, and unto God the things that are God's." To understand which it may not be improper to observe, that Judea had lately become a Roman province; and though, in general, permitted to be governed by its own laws, and to enjoy the exercise of the national religion, confessed its allegiance by submitting to the appointment of a Roman governor, or nominal king, the payment of public tribute, and an appeal, in the last resort, to Cæsar. The Jews, dissatisfied with their new master, as might be naturally looked for, bore the yoke with extreme impatience. They, therefore, propose a question, probably devised to insinuate their dissatisfaction with the authority which the Roman empire had assumed, certainly to ensnare Jesus, and to expose him to the resentment of the civil powers by the answer which they expected from him.—Mark with what address they introduce themselves, " Master we know that thou art true, and teachest the way of God in truth, neither carest thou for any man, tell us, therefore, is it lawful to give tribute to Cæsar or not?" What a fine compliment this, and how artfully formed to throw one off his guard. They would seem to acknowledge his claim to a divine character, and such an unlimited confidence in his authority, as to be finally determined by his decision of the question; but well knowing their insidious intentions, with admirable justness and propriety, he returned the following answer: " But Jesus perceived their wickedness, and said, why tempt ye me ye hypocrites, show me the tribute money;—whose is this image and superscription? And they said, Cæsar's: then saith he unto them, render unto Cæsar the things that are Cæsar's, and unto God the things that are God's." This money is a plain proof of the authority of the Roman empire: it bears the image of Cæsar as your sovereign, and your admitting it as the lawful and current coin of this country, is an implicit acknowledgment of his authority in civil and temporal articles: neither can ye plead conscience, with any consistency, in refusing to pay it: political constitutions are daily exposed to changes, and are obliged to submit to great innovations: this is the order of Providence, which pulls down one state and raises up another, seemingly at pleasure, but, in truth, for wise and important reasons, of which we can sometimes, but more frequently cannot possibly judge. It is the wise order of Providence, in particular, with regard to you, as now a dependent nation and people;—and as to the paying tribute, it is in itself an indifferent thing, and may be lawfully paid under one form of government as well as another.— While the civil powers, therefore, do not transgress their proper limits, and assume a right of violating the sacred obligations of conscience, never pretend to call in question those duties that arise from the dependence

of

of a subject, and the circumstances in which he is unavoidably placed.—But, if *these* should at any time be invaded, remember you must render to God the things that are God's; seeing no human tribunal has a right to determine for another, where the question is, what am I to believe concerning God, or what is that worship which he requires, and is alone acceptable to him? Every thing in this question is an appeal to man, as a rational and moral being, and he is accountable to God only.—If this comment appear just, the reader, it is hoped, will excuse the length of it, as it contains an explicit declaration, from the highest authority, concerning the rights of conscience, and the duty we owe as subjects to civil government.

Let us now enquire, in the *second* place, whether the sacred writings leave the rights of conscience and private judgment entire, as members of *Christian* society?— Whether they constitute any spiritual guide, or any particular order of men, with paramount and exclusive powers of direction over the conscience, and decision in matters of faith?—Or whether they appeal to the collective body of Christians, in general, and every individual, in particular, as having a right, from the nature of their character as men, and the religion proposed to them ;—founded upon proper evidence, and implying a personal interest ;—to think, to enquire, to judge for themselves.

When the Saviour of the world appeared in the exercise of his public character, the simple question was— " Art thou he that should come, or do we look for another?"

ther?" Now there was no way of determining this question with any certainty, but by an appeal to the Scriptures of the old Testament concerning him, or by some evidence he was to exhibit of himself, or both — With regard to the *first*, as by the Scriptures his real character was to be determined, to the Scriptures he directs the inquiry of his hearers, and calls upon every individual to search and judge for himself, even in opposition to *Church* authority, which was exercised, at that time, as it hath been in every age where it hath assumed a dominion over the conscience, without regard to truth or humanity — " They bind heavy burdens and grievous to be borne, and lay them on men's shoulders, but they themselves will not move them with one of their fingers." He, therefore, warns the people on all occasions against the imposition of these arrogant guides, however clothed with the most venerable names of Rabbis, Doctors, Elders,—of the synagogue, or sanhedrim, " Call no man master upon earth;" and he never fails to lead them back to the law, and to direct them to an impartial inquiry *there*, when through false glosses, and artificial interpretations put upon it, he perceived their understanding had been misled, and their sense of divine things grosly corrupted.

WITH regard to the *second*, the evidence our Lord exhibited of his divine character — the miracles which he wrought, the doctrines which he taught, and, in general the conformity of his whole appearance to his publick mission — all these were exposed to publick view and examination. His miracles were wrought openly, and a fair opportunity afforded of publick and private inquiry

quiry—" thefe things were not done in a corner." His doctrines were delivered to the multitude, and were unfolded gradually as they were able to bear, or to underſtand them. As he aſſumed the character of a teacher come from God, ſo he improved every opportunity of divine inſtruction, removing prejudices, and furniſhing every means of conviction.— Hence he tells them, " If I had not come and ſpoken unto you ye had been without ſin, but now ye have no cloak for your ſin." He no where attempts to ſubſtitute authority, not even the higheſt, in the place of evidence; but reaſons with his hearers as moral and intelligent beings, who, therefore, had a juſt claim to demand ſatisfaction with regard to the grounds of their faith. He doth not, even overlook the objections of his moſt unreaſonable oppoſers, and moſt inveterate enemies, but anſwers them on their own principles, with a clearneſs and energy, that nothing but the moſt invincible prejudices could poſſibly reſiſt.—In one word, on the evidence which he exhibited; ſo as to render all inexcuſable, he reſts the whole deciſion of his public character, " If any man hear my words and believe not, I judge him not; he hath one that judgeth him, the word that I have ſpoken, the ſame ſhall judge him in the laſt day."

THE Apoſtles who were immediately commiſſioned by their Divine Maſter, follow the ſame plan. They had received no authoritative power over the conſciences of men. They were commanded ſimply to teach; and for this end were inſtructed in all the laws of his ſpiritual kingdom, and all the doctrines of the new diſpenſation they were called to eſtabliſh — Agreeably to this

commiſſion

commission they explain, in different points of view, and enforce the distinguishing tenets of Christianity from the most convincing arguments, directing those to whom they address themselves to personal inquiry, so as to be able to give a reason of the hope that was in them; and on all occasions, while they alarm the conscience, they convince the judgment. There were early pretenders to Apostolic powers. What course were christians to take? were they to compare the *spirits* together, aud to judge from *their* characters and doctrine? were they to judge from what their understandings might suggest, assisted by any more perfect rule of which they might be in possession? or were they to appeal to *church* authority? There was no such standard as *church* authority in those days. They were to judge for themselves by the best means with which Providence had furnished them. " Believe not every spirit but try the spirits whether they are of God, for many false spirits are gone out into the world," a caution and direction that must have been interpreted as the cruelest of all insults, if they had no right to inquire and judge for themselves—But that a spirit of honest inquiry was accounted not only a laudable temper of mind, but necessary to lay a solid and rational foundation for the faith of christians to rest upon, appears with the most convincing evidence from the high eulogy which the sacred historian makes on the Bereans. " These were more noble than those in Thessalonica, in that they received the word with all readiness of mind, and searched the Scriptures daily, whether these things were so or not." They received nothing upon report, or mere authority—even Apostolical, but searched the Scriptures of the Old Testament, com-

paring

paring them with the doctrines of the New, and found that they supported and mutually illustrated one another. Noble Bereans indeed! but how unhappy would your fate have been, had your lot fallen in days of church authority; ye would have been denounced heretics, and piously consigned to the flames.

If ever any man had a claim to authority in the churches, the Apostle Paul was he: his call was extraordinary, the means of his instruction were extraordinary, his learning and address were extraordinary, and his influence among the churches was very great. But doth he at any time employ *this* authority, or the influence he had so justly acquired to check a spirit of inquiry, or to overawe the conscience? His views were very different, " Moreover I call God for a record upon my soul, that to spare you I came not as yet to Corinth." He had used all the plainness, and all the prudent severity that became a wise instructor, a tender spiritual father. He had reproved their errors, and admonished them for their faults, he had set their danger before them, and given them his best advice—in which he aimed at no authority, but what arose from their conviction of the truth, and their sense of having been in the wrong. He durst go no further. " Not that we have dominion over your faith, but are helpers of your joy." And he gives an excellent reason for his not attempting so injurious an usurpation—a reason that ought to have precluded every future attempt of this kind; " For by faith ye stand."—Your faith is your security amidst all the dangers to which ye must be exposed on account of your profession, and amidst all temptations arising from

F 4   sensible

sensible objects, by which ye are in hazard of being seduced; it ought not, therefore, to be blind faith: your convictions, the grounds on which your hopes are formed ought to be rational, and the effect of the most impartial and satisfying inquiry: ye ought to be fully persuaded in your own minds independently of any personal authority of mine. It were endless to quote passages in support of the rights of conscience and private judgment; they are innumerable; and we may defy all the sons of Levi to produce one single text, from whence it shall appear that the inspired penmen have established a select junto to judge authoritatively of their writings, have directed any part of them to an order of *Ecclesiastics* to be explained only by them—or finally, that they have established any human jurisdiction to which we are subjected, and by which our opinions and actions are cogzible as moral and accountable beings—The Scriptures are evidently directed to the whole body of christians, or to different christian societies as representative of them. By these societies they were read and studied, no man pretending to dominion over another; not even those immediately commissioned by the Apostles. They would not claim what their constituents had formally disclaimed. Their work was to feed the flock of God, and to be examples to it, to admonish them in the spirit of love and meekness, and not to lord it over God's heritage: they desired no more—Holding the truth in unrighteousness or an obstinate opposition to the dictates of conscience, by which the offender stood evidently self condemned, constituted, in those days of Apostolic simplicity, the idea of an *heretic*, and was the capital ground of public censure.

BUT

But why do we appeal to any particular difpenfation? The great Lord of the univerfe, in the general order of Providence, doth not deal with his rational creatures by mere authority, but agreeably to their moral and intelligent natures—If, in particular inftances, he hath concealed the immediate end he had in view, or the propriety of the means for accomplifhing it; if he hath done this to teach men fubmiffion, and to preferve upon their minds a fenfe of their own imperfection, and entire dependence upon him, it is becaufe, on the whole, he hath given them the fulleft evidence and ftrongeft conviction that his ways are juft and equal. " Judge, I pray you, betwext me my and vineyard, what more would have been done to my vineyard that I have not done in it?" Thus he condefcends to appeal to the reafon and the confciences of men, and permits his ways to be tried at that bar, in thofe inftances where his moral adminiftration is properly the object of thofe powers—And can we fuppofe, that he hath entrufted any created being with an authority, which his own perfections, and the faculties by which he hath diftinguifhed the nature of man, will not permit him to exercife? It cannot be fuppofed without the higheft impiety and abfurdity.

SECT. IV.

Of the capacity of the greater part of judging for themfelves.

WHAT hath been offered in fupport of the rights of private judgment, may, perhaps, appear to fome some as mere speculation—an idle philosophical reverie in direct opposition to fact and experience. And, by such, it will, no doubt, be urged, that a religion deriving its chief credit from authority, in whatever contempt it may be held in theory, hath been, and will continue to be the religion of the multitude in every age and country; that the greater part are not formed nor placed in circumstances for examination; especially where tedious researches, deep disquisitions, and critical inquiry are necessary to ascertain the precise idea and meaning of the author, and where men of learning and great abilities differ among themselves; that this holds true, in particular with regard to the Scriptures, especially Paul's epistles, where the sense is often obscure, and the reasoning broken by long digressions; that, in such circumstances, we cannot suppose that the bulk of mankind are capable of personal inquiry, and judging for themselves.

This it must be acknowledged, is plausibly enough urged, because it seems to rest upon, and to derive its chief force from the general circumstances of mankind; but a little attention will satisfy every man of common understanding, that there is no real weight in in it—For

First, the ignorance of the bulk of mankind is not owing to incapacity, or the disadvantageous circumstances in which they are placed; but, more generally, to a most criminal inattention to every moral and religious concern.—Men are early taught, and soon learn from experience, that every occupation, art, or science, requires time, labour, and attention to arrive at any perfection in it; and, therefore, never think of becoming artists,

artists, or scholars, without proper application: but, with regard to religion, they see almost every one disposed to trust to accident, or to some spiritual guide, whom they have been accustomed to consider as led by their trade to make the proper inquiry; and as they have not observed any sensible inconvenience arising from this manner of adopting a creed, they can perceive no necessity of leaving the beaten tract, or giving themselves any further trouble about the matter. They are well satisfied with the religion of their fathers, or the sect whose tenets they have been taught from their infancy to hold sacred: and thus a particular mode of religion becomes a family distinction, and is faithfully transmitted from father to son without examination, or knowing any thing further on the subject than certain names and forms that mark different contending parties. Hence, whatever talents or abilities men are possessed of in other respects, few ever think of becoming wiser, or receiving any improvement in their religious knowledge. The defect arises not, therefore, from want of understanding, but from inattention — For it will be found, I apprehend, that the understandings of men are more on a level, than is commonly imagined, where they have the same motives to consideration and inquiry; and however learning may serve to lay open new sources of knowledge, it will never make that understanding distinct and vigorous, which was before incorrect and feeble. It may enlarge the sphere of our ideas, and give the mind a wider compass to range in; but that power which adopts or rejects first principles, which perceives the agreement or disagreement between ideas, which connects or separates them, and leads us to certain conclusions, must

have

have been antecedently the gift of nature, and cannot fail to discover itself, when a subject is fairly proposed, and rendered in any measure interesting to us.—Let us suppose, for instance, that every individual were as much convinced, that it was necessary for him to understand the New Testament, as to be acquainted with a deed, conveying to him a fortune, or legacy of great value, but left him on this sole condition, that he should be able to read and explain the capital articles contained in it; and what would be the consequence? It might be pronounced with assurance, that there are few, in such a case, that would not be able to give a tolerable account of it. For,

Secondly, it is by no means true, that the New Testament is so unintelligible, even to ordinary understandings, as is pretended.—Nothing could be more injurious to the moral perfections of God, than to suppose, that he should have given a rule of duty not to be understood by those for whom it was intended. It would be to suppose the Deity acting below the standard of common sense and common humanity. It ought, therefore, to be maintained, and it is certainly fact, that the Scriptures, with regard to the great and leading doctrines and precepts contained in them, are plain, and may be understood by every individual of common capacity, who is truly disposed to pay due attention to them.— Many things, indeed, may appear dark and intricate; they do so to men of the greatest capacity and learning. What then? Doth not the natural world abound with difficulties which no human understanding can resolve? But will it follow from thence, that the works of the

great

great Creator were not intended to difplay, and do not actually difplay his glory; that, notwithftanding thefe difficulties, which puzzle the human underftanding, they do not exhibit the cleareft, and moft convincing proof of fupreme intelligence, wifdom, and goodnefs? The Scriptures, therefore, in perfect analogy to the general order of Providence, may contain many things hard to be underftood, and which they that are unftable and unlearned wreft to their own deftruction, and yet may exhibit a fyftem of doctrines, as a rule of faith, and of duties and precepts, as a rule of life and conduct, adapted to the capacities of all.—Obfervation and experience have been daily contributing their aids in throwing new light on fome of the moft obfcure paffages; and, no doubt, ftill additional light will be thrown on parts yet hid from us, as it fhall be fubfervient to the great defigns of divine wifdom, in gradually unfolding his moral plan; when things that no human underftanding could have difcovered, will appear fufficiently plain.—In the mean time, no man is accountable further than his underftanding can penetrate, and and he has the opportunities of enquiry; if he hath not wilfully neglected the means of improvement, and arriving at the knowledge of the truth. If he ufes the advantages he enjoys, if he fearches with candour, if he acts with honefty, he has nothing to fear. He has much to hope. He has reafon to believe, that he fhall not fall into any dangerous miftake. " If any man do his will, he fhall know of the doctrine, whether it be of God or not." That honefty of heart, and uprightnefs of temper, which leads to a confcientious performance of duty, fo far as it is known, is the beft prefervative

againft

against error, into which men are more frequently led by a bad disposition and irregular passions, than the weakness of their understandings.

It may be thought that the difficulty of ascertaining whether the originals are faithfully transmitted and translated, must still remain an invincible draw-back against the unlearned judging for themselves. But one observation is sufficient to remove every difficulty on this article, and give perfect ease to the understanding —That without supposing the whole body of the learned uniting in one common design of imposing upon those who cannot examine into the originals with their own eyes, there can be no possible deception in this matter; which, considering the distance of countries, and ages, separate interests, and the opposition of different religious parties, is morally impossible. The unlearned, therefore, have all the security their hearts can desire concerning every thing of importance in Christianity. They have more security for the authenticity of the scriptures, and the genuine sense of the originals, where a spirit of liberal examination is permitted, than that the translation of any other book on earth exhibits fairly the sentiments of its author—Amidst all the various translations of the sacred volumes, and all the variety of deep and ingenious criticisms, so far as we are acquainted with them, there still remains a unity sufficient to direct our faith and morals, and that truly may be said to leave the capital doctrines and duties of Christianity unaffected.

But *thirdly*, if it should be admitted that many by themselves are incapable of understanding the Scriptures,

tures, what, should hinder private Christians of weaker capacities from the advantage of those friendly aids that are freely offered to them from all quarters — the labours of men of clear heads, great erudition, and honest hearts, who seem evidently to have searched the truth for its own sake, who never once entertained a thought of making a monopoly of the Scriptures, or establishing their own judgments into a public standard; and who were incapable of the wickedness, had it been in their power, of rearing up a spiritual jurisdiction on the ignorance, credulity, and superstition of mankind? While such friendly aids remain, the most ignorant may be instructed, and, if they are truly disposed, arrive at some confidence in their own minds that " these things are so."

But learned and good men may differ. So they may, and so they do, and it is of importance that they should: because those points in which they agree, and which, as hath been just now observed, are the capital doctrines and duties of Christianity, are hereby rendered more certain, and free from every suspicion of fraud and design.—Now while these doctrines and duties are universally acknowledged, every honest man of a plain understanding may certainly determine, from *their* nature and tendency, the real spirit and genius of Christianity, and may thereby be enabled, in a great measure, to fix a test by which he may satisfy his own mind, concerning differences of lesser importance that may happen among the learned —— But if, after all, private Christians should on some occasions be at a loss to arrive at certainty amidst contending parties, there is no remedy; they

must

must make the best use of their understandings they can, and rest there. For who doth not see that it is infinitely preferable to submit to a partial evil, than to establish a general rule that would destroy liberty of inquiry altogether, with regard to those who had capacity and opportunities, without furnishing those who had neither with one degree of more certainty as to the grounds of their faith; but, on the contrary, would expose both learned and unlearned, wise men and fools, to every error and superstitious delusion, that would most effectually answer the purposes of those ecclesiastics, who, under pretence of divine authority, had assumed the leading of their understandings and consciences.

It is of no purpose to say, that still the weak and the ignorant would be directed in their creed, and led by somebody: because, supposing the fact, it is a voluntary submission. It is a submission that arises, or is supposed to arise from their own choice. They are bound down by no coercive power, nor obliged to receive, under the terror of the most dreadful penal sanctions *here*, and damnation *hereafter*, whatever opinions or practices may be stamped with *church* authority, and injuriously obtruded upon them. What they assent to this day, upon further inquiry, and better information, they may retract to-morrow; and are under no restraint, but what arises from the free exercise of their intellectual powers, and the genuine dictates of their own consciences.—This is RELIGIOUS LIBERTY, which, next to the proper improvement of it, is the most valuable blessing that heaven can bestow on man.

SECT.

SECT. V.

OF RELIGIOUS ORDER.

THERE is not any thing that seems to be less understood than *order* in religion. In its general idea, it is supposed to include *uniformity* with regard to certain articles of faith, and a certain mode of external worship. This is a notion that *priests* in every age and country have been at the utmost pains to inculcate. *Here* they have exhausted much eloquence, while they have declaimed in all the rage of holy indignation against heresy, schism, sectarism, free thinking, and all the myriads of evils that spring from divisions in religion. Nor is it to be wondered at, that they should. It is one of the most successful engines of their craft—For this uniformity of opinions, and mode of worship, being impossible if men are left to consult the Scriptures, and their own understandings, or to form a judgment from the best helps that their opportunities in life can furnish; it follows that some public establishment is necessary, by which common articles of faith, and a common ritual ought to be defined and ascertained; and who is able, or who hath a right in an article so sacred —but the *church?*

THAT the Romanists should have availed themselves of this sort of reasoning, with those who were weak and superstitious enough to be satisfied with it, is by no means matter of surprise; and they are, at least consistent fiftent with themfelves: but that it ever fhould have entered into the head of proteftants, is aftonifhing; becaufe, if the argument be good for any thing, it is good for eftablifhing an univerfal fpiritual monarchy; and there it would infalliby iffue, if thofe who are poffeffed of fuch notions of religious order, as to brand all that differ from them with odious epithets, were vefted with adequate powers.

WHAT hath led men into this pernicious miftake, feems in a great meafure, to have been the ftating an analogy between religion and civil government, where, in this point of view, there is no analogy at all—A certain, determined, order is neceffary in civil government to the very exiftence of it, becaufe, a conformity to certain external regulations being the foundation of its fecurity and prefervation, muft neceffarily be the grand object of its cognizance; fo that he who enjoys the benefit and protection of the laws, and yet pretends to act in oppofition to them, is properly a *diforderly* fubject; but with regard to religion the cafe is quite different. Order here hath little dependence upon the externals of any kind, and fuch externals as conftitute this order extend no further, as a law, than the fentiments of the fmalleft religious focieties, fhould it be but two or three in the name of Chrift, that may affemble for worfhip. The order of religion is a *moral* order. It is the order of a good heart, and a converfation becoming the Gofpel—Order, if it carry any idea at all in it, is the proper arrangement and relation of certain parts, as thefe parts are connected with a particular end or defign: nothing, therefore, can be diforderly with regard

gard to that end which is moſt ſubſervient in promoting it. Now in religion, beyond all doubt, the great end is approving ovrſelves to God; and the means moſt ſubſervient to this end—doing his will. Hence he is the moſt *orderly* chriſtian who is at the greateſt pains to know the will of God, and moſt conſcientious in performing it.

But though order, as denoting *uniformity*, can never become national, nor prevail to any conſiderable degree, where men are left to the free exerciſe of their underſtandings—unawed by Eccleſiaſtic terrors—unbribed by public rewards; ſtill there will be found union ſufficient to form little ſocieties, connected by common opinions, one common mode of worſhip, or ſome more general principles, who reſting, each upon their own bottom, could never think, conſiſtently with themſelves, of aſſuming an authority over, or pretending to dictate to one another.

But ſuppoſing what variety in religious ſentiments and modes of worſhip you pleaſe, may it not be modeſtly aſked, what harm, what real injury to ſociety or individuals can ariſe from this variety? Are any of thoſe laws violated on which the publick welfare depends? Is there any uſurpation attempted upon the property, the underſtanding, or conſcience of another? Is any man his brother's keeper, or is he accountable for him? To theſe queſtions it ſurely may be anſwered with great confidence—that, if the ſubject be confined wholly to religion, there can be no harm at all, no injury to public or private happineſs. " If thou doſt well ſhalt thou not be accepted? And if thou doſt not well, ſin lieth at the door." Worldly ends and the means neceſſary for accompliſhing them may juſtle together, becauſe thoſe means are very limited, and the point we aim at, if occupied by one, cannot be poſſeſſed by another: hence a thouſand accidents may every day occur to produce jealouſies and oppoſition: but what ſhould diſturb one man about the religious ſentiments of another—where, if the means ſhould differ, or if they ſhould agree, they do not interfere with one another—where, they may differ and the ſame end be obtained? What, but an intolerating ſpirit, the effect of a mind contracted by the moſt illiberal prejudices; what, but an arrogance of ſoul, the effect of intellectual pride, rendered fierce by ſuppoſed oppoſition; what, but the luſt of ſpiritual dominion, the effect of *prieſtly* policy ſhould awaken animoſity and ill nature *here?* " We are actuated by no ſuch illiberal views: no animoſity, no ill nature. We are prompted by a warm ſenſibility—a generous concern for the beſt intereſts of our fellow men. Can we ſee them expoſed to ſuch imminent danger—wandering in the paths of error and ready to periſh, without one friendly emotion, or one endeavour to reclaim them? What you moſt uncharitably call prejudice, policy, pride, and fierceneſs of temper, is truly the overflowing of a benevolent heart, touched with a ſenſe of human miſery—that would " have compaſſion, pulling them out of the fire." What ſurprizing care do theſe patrons of *religious order* take of other peoples conſciences! This is ſurely amazingly generous and kind hearted; and it were a pity not to permit them to lend their beſt aſſiſtance, and to adminiſter their kindeſt offices

fices — Well, be it so: but let me ask in what manner would ye gratify these very tender feelings? " We would convert schismatics of every denomination to the purity of faith and worship — one faith, one Lord, one baptism;" *that is,* you would endeavour to make them think just as you do: quite right. But by what means? " We would be at all pains to convince them by reason, by argument, by informing their understandings and removing every conscientious scruple — We would weep over them, we would pray for them." Still excellent — But if after all your pious labours they should remain obstinate schismatics, would you proceed one step further? You are silent, and so far you are honest; for you cannot fairly consult your own hearts and say you would not. No man knows where he is to stop, once he begins to meddle with the religious opinions of another; because the very attempt must proceed from want of that candour — that charity and enlargement of mind which is formed by rational inquiry, and a real conviction of the truth. Such have been led to believe through accident; and they can perceive no reason why others should not believe in the same manner. They depend not, therefore, upon argument but authority. If you see with their eyes, it is well; but if you will use your own, you may be fully assured, that the severity of penal laws, if the power shall be unhappily lodged in their hands, will convince you of your obstinacy — Or if they can go no further, they will show what manner of spirit they are of, by giving you fairly over to the devil, so far as their interest goes — In vain, therefore, do these patrons of religious uniformity talk of liberty, of conscience, of reason and argument.

gument. They are at bottom the enemies of conscience and private judgment — Their sympathy is all grimace — Their tears would bring tears of blood from the eyes of those they pretend to pity — Their admonitions would be more wounding than the sting of a serpent — and their prayers but a gloomy prelude to the flames.

CHAP. IV.

OF THE CHURCH.

SECT I.

OF THE IDEA OF A CHRISTIAN CHURCH.

AS this term hath been made use of in the preceding chapters as generally understood by ecclesiastics, for an order of men, not only distinguished from particular christian societies, but the collective body of christians;—an order of men supposed to be possessed of certain exclusive spiritual powers; we shall now endeavour to fix the genuine meaning of it from the sacred writings.

IF we look into the gospels, we find the word not mentioned but on two different occasions. The *one* is, where our Lord refers the case of contending parties to the church, " If thy brother neglect to hear thee tell it to the church:" and here it is sufficiently plain, either that the ordinary forms of decision in the Jewish ecclesiastic courts are intended, or the particular religious community, of which the person offending was an immediate member. Before one or other of *these*, the complaining party was to bring his cause, and expect redress.—The last, however, seems to have been the method approved of by the Apostle, of deciding controversies among the primitive Christians; " I speak to your

your shame, is there not a wise man among you, not one who shall be able to judge between his brother, but brother goeth to law with brother, and that before the unbelievers." But whether this reference was to be made to the sanhedrim or the synagogue, it makes no difference. It can throw no light upon our inquiry into the nature and constitution of a christian church.

The *other* passage, where this word occurs, deserves a little more attention; "And I say unto thee, thou art Peter, and on this rock will I build *my* church." Here, it must be acknowledged, that Christ evidently points to the constitution of a *Christian* church; and it is well known what a handle the Romanists make of these words;—presumptuously pretending, that Peter is here vested with the sole headship of the church of Christ, with the exclusive right of the *keys*; and thence deriving the exorbitant and impious claims of the Pope.— But, how is it possible for one to determine any thing with certainty from this general declaration, supposing the purpose to have been of building a church upon Peter? A thousand different conjectures, as the fancy or views of individuals should lead them, might be formed concerning this church and its foundation; but no man of a sound understanding, or honest heart, would pretend to affirm, that, from this single passage, any decisive conclusion could be deduced, in support of any particular model or constitution of church government.

But, perhaps, the history of Peter, in other parts of the sacred writings, may clear up, and direct us in, this matter. *There* we *may* be more particularly informed what

what pre-eminence he had above the other Apoſtles, and by what peculiar powers he was diſtinguiſhed; what regulations he hath left concerning the eſtabliſhment and government of a chriſtian church, to whom he hath bequeathed his paramount powers, by what particular characters his ſucceſſors are marked out, and in what manner the ſucceſſion is to be carried forward and perpetuated. All this had been very well, and would have certainly ended the difpute; but there happens unluckily no ſuch inſtructions to be found; not one hint of one or other of theſe particulars in his own epiſtles, nor in any part of the book of God. We read of no pre-eminence, no delegated powers, no eſtabliſhed ſucceſſion, no model of a chriſtian church, no fixed ſtandard, by which the order and diſcipline of it was to be conducted. So that conſidering the paſſage, as having an immediate reference to the conſtitution of a chriſtian church built on the authority given to Peter;—it leaves us without ideas altogether.

But there is another view, in which it is commonly underſtood among proteſtants, that has a plain, ſenſible, and pertinent meaning;—that by the rock on which Chriſt was to build his church, our Lord intends the particular doctrine which Peter expreſſed in his confeſſion, and which he declares fleſh and blood had not revealed to him. In this ſenſe, whatever is intended by *my church*, the foundation of it was to be laid in the belief and acknowledgment of this propoſition, "*That Chriſt is the Son of the living God;*" for this is the very acknowledgment or confeſſion which our Lord takes notice of, and immediately aſcribes to a higher original

nal than flesh and blood.—Wherever, therefore, this capital article is believed, and openly expressed in the sense in which Peter expresses it, and the New Testament explains it;—there doth the church of Christ exist in its original purity.—Every distinct society professing this faith, is a distinct church; and the whole body of believers taken together is the church universal, or catholic, redeemed by his blood.

It hath been observed by a late author, that Christ *here*, more probably refers to Peter's testimony, or his evidence as a witness, than to his confession—as if he had said, "I constitute thee Peter a witness, and upon this testimony of thine I will build my church." But with all due deference to the superior erudition of this writer; we cannot possibly conceive the propriety or justice of this explication; because there is evidently a *speciality* intended in this passage, and there appears nothing peculiar to Peter as a witness of his Lord—Besides, the church of Christ is built, not on the testimony of one Apostle, but on the foundation of the prophets and apostles; on the collective evidence that arises from the old and new dispensation.—But there is one truth that lies at the foundation of Christianity, and without which it hath no existence, "that Christ is the son of the living God;" and therefore the apostolic writings resolve the whole of Christianity into the belief of it: "Whosoever shall confess that Jesus is the son of God, God dwelleth in him, and he in God—He that believeth on the son of God hath the witness in himself—That is the word of faith which we preach, that if thou shalt confess with thy mouth the Lord Jesus, and shalt believe

in

in thine heart that God raised him from the dead, thou shalt be saved — Whoso believeth that Jesus is the Christ is born of God." This truth, therefore, may be justly considered as the rock intended by our Lord. And, indeed, what can be a more significant symbol of it than a rock — an immoveable security and defence — a hiding place from the wind — a covert from the tempest — a refreshing shadow in a weary land? A stone erected into a pillar, or stones piled into a heap, it is acknowledged were anciently used as memorials of personal covenants and mercies as well as public transactions; and seem to have been continued in one or other of these views from the first ages to monuments that still remain; and therefore may be allowed to be proper symbols of testimony; but a rock leads us to the justest idea of this grand truth, on which all our hopes as Christians are founded. And are not the foundations of the Christian's hope, and the foundations of the Christian church the same? Our Lord, therefore, assures Peter, that the belief of this truth should in all ages unite his followers into one body, be the common object of their hope and joy, and render them, in opposition to all the instruments and designs of hell, impregnable like a rock.

SECT. II.

Of the Conformity of this Idea of a Christian Church to the Apostolic Doctrine.

THE number of christian converts who assembled together after our Lord's resurrection were one hundred and twenty. Soon after, by means of Peter's preaching, there thousand souls were added, so that the whole

whole christian society, at time, amounted to three thousand one hundred and twenty, who, "continuing daily with one acccord in the temple, and breaking bread from house to house, did eat their meat with gladness and singleness of heart, praising God." What is subjoined by the sacred historian deserves attention—"And the Lord added daily to the church such as should be saved." Can words be more explicit to ascertain the Apostolic idea of a christian church? For of whom, possibly, can the writer speak but of these three thousand one hundred and twenty? These converts, therefore, taken together were, at that time, the church of Christ: and as the number of believers encreased, the church became enlarged in her collective capacity. But in proportion to her encrease, different and distinct societies were of course formed, disjoined from one another by countries and seas—sometimes consisting of many, more frequently of few members. To hold correspondence with one another, much more to meet in one common assembly was impossible. It was necessary therefore, that whatever rights belonged to the common body, should likewise belong to these separate societies—Accordingly, however small and inconsiderable, if united together in the name, and as professing disciples of Christ, these societies are always considered, and addressed as a christian church. If any one who hath read the Apostolic writings could be supposed ignorant of this, let him attend to the following passages: "As for Saul he made havock of the *church*, entering into every house, and hauling men and women, committed them to prison." Here it is evident, that by the church is meant the body of christians in general, who were thus
miserable

miserably harassed in their separate societies and retreats by this bloody persecutor, so that hardly an individual could assure himself of safety—" And it came to pass that they (Paul and Barnabas) assembled themselves a whole year with the *church* at Antioch, and the disciples were called christians first at Antioch." It is no less plain from this passage, that these christians who first met together for religious worship at Antioch in the name of Christ, and from which they were denominated chrstians, are called the church: and it is to be carefully noted that they do not receive this description on account of Paul and Barnabas joining their society; for *they* are said expresly to have assembled *themselves* with the church. Besides, neither of these had, at this time received any special commission as public ministers of christianity—" Unto whom not only I give thanks but the *churches* among the Gentiles," that is the different christian societies scattered among the Gentiles " likewise greet the *church* that is in their house (the house of Aquila and Priscilla) " salute Nymphas and the *church* that is in the house — Paul unto Philemon, and the *church* that is in his house." It is not certain even, whether by the church in the three last passages is to be understood more than the very members of the family. However this be, many might be quoted to prove, beyond doubt, that the Apostles always consider a society of christians, whether larger or smaller professedly met to worship in the name of Jesus Christ, as a christian church.

In confirmation of this account, it is to be observed, that there is not one suggestion in all the new testament, that

that the Apostles or Elders, or any denomination of ecclesiastic officers, constituted the church. On the contrary, they are evidently distinguished from the church, and consulted on momentous occasions with it.

When the great controversy arose concerning certain observances which the Jewish converts would have imposed upon those of the Gentiles, and the question became warm, delegates were immediately dispatched from Antioch to Jerusalem to consult with the *church* there about this weighty matter; " And when they were to come to Jerusalem they were received of the *church*, and the *Apostles* aud *Elders*." Who does not see that the church is here considered as a distinct body from the Apostles and Elders? Again, " Then pleased it the Apostles and Elders with the whole *church* to send chosen men of their own company with Paul and Barnabas to Antioch, and wrote letters to them after this manner—The Apostles and Elders and Brethren (or Church) send greeting." Is it possible for words to render it more plain, that the church in those days consisted, not of Apostles or Elders, or of Ecclesiastic officers of any kind met together to deliberate concerning doctrine or discipline, but in the society and fellowship of christians professing one common faith, and joining together in love and charity in common acts of worship.

As christians thus assembled were always denominated the *church*; so the Apostles consider *them* as having a common right to determine in every important question. Accordingly, when the point concerning circumcision came to be maturely deliberated upon, instead of taking the decision decifion of it entirely upon themfelves in virtue of their peculiar powers, the Apoftles and Elders confulted with, and act agreeably to the common voice of the chriftian fociety or *church*: "Then pleafed it the Apoftles and Elders with the whole *church*."—As a further proof that the primitive minifters of religion acted in concert with the fociety of chriftians in every matter of public concern, it may be remarked, that when the anfwer to be returned to the *church* at Antioch was finally agreed upon, and they had refolved to fend two of their own number, Paul and Barnabas, to report the decifion, they faw it proper to join in the commiffion with them, "Judas and Silas chofen men among the brethren," that it might appear to be the common determination of the Apoftles, Elders, and the *Church*—So cautious feem even thofe extraordinary minifters to have been, of giving the leaft fufpicion of affuming a dominion over the faith of chriftians. Whatever powers, therefore, the church of Chrift may be poffeffed of, they belong *radically* to every chriftian fociety affembled for the great purpofe of promoting the interefts of religion—private or public edification, fo far as they are animated by the fpirit of Chriftianity, and directed by the laws of it—it being impoffible that the whole body of chriftians fhould at any time, the firft church excepted, have united in one common fociety.

SECT.

SECT. III.

OF THE APOSTLES AND ELDERS.

A QUESTION will probably arife from what hath been advanced on this fubject that claims fome attention. What then were the apoftles and elders? Did they hold no fuperior rank, and were they vefted with no fpecial powers as diftinguifhed from the body of Chriftians in general? They certainly held a fuperior rank. They certainly were endowed with extraordinary powers, and were authorifed by an extraordinary mandate. The Apoftles were chofen as witneffes for their Lord, and were honoured to lay open his divine embaffy in all its extent: but as the grand truths, and moft comfortable doctrines of Chriftianity depend upon events, which, though often hinted at, and, on fome occafions, exprefsly foretold by their Divine Mafter, they could not be brought to believe, his fufferings, death, and refurrection; and, as it was neceffary that thefe events fhould take place before the ineftimable bleffings founded upon them fhould be exhibited and explained, it was not till our Lord actually rofe from the grave that his Apoftles were furnifhed with evidence, and endowed with fuitable powers to execute their commiffion. This commiffion they firft opened on the day pentecoft; and by addreffing themfelves to a numerous affembly of different nations and languages — to every one in his own tongue, and by preaching "Jefus that he was the Chrift" now rifen from the dead, and remiffion of fins by him, they were enabled

abled to lay the foundation of the christian church.—And from their whole history it appears, that their peculiar work lay in unfolding the plan of the gospel, converting unbelievers to the faith, and forming distinct christian societies, or churches, in the course of their pious and succesful labours; and of which they themselves were the spiritual fathers, instructors, and guides, so long as they could remain among them, and had opportunity to correspond with them.—But though the Apostles were the first planters of the christian vineyard, yet they were not equal to the task of extending it in every quarter, and of watering it in every corner. Their instructions were highly necessary as a general and public standard, but they were not alone sufficient in every exigence. For this purpose subsidiary aids were appointed; men of distinguished piety and wisdom, and qualified by miraculous and extraordinary powers, to superintend the spiritual concerns of different christian societies. These were the elders of whom we so frequently read, who are particularly distinguished from the Apostles, as appears from the embassy sent from Jerusalem to Antioch in the passage above quoted; and who evidently bore an inferior office: being either appointed by the Apostles themselves, or by others, having an immediate commission for that purpose.—These again were men who held a middle class between the Apostles and Elders, and who accompanied and assisted them in their itinerary labours; of which number were Timothy and Titus, of whom we shall have occasion to speak afterwards. — Besides these, there were prophets and teachers, whose commission and powers were more limited. But all of them, whether apostles, elders, evangelists, prophets, or teachers, were extraordinary ministers, and furnished with different gifts suited to the particular sphere in which they were called to act.—Indeed, without such a multiplicity of gifts, those infant societies could have never been preserved amidst so many dangers, nor fortified amidst so many and great trials: for, besides persecution from the established church, and the civil powers prompted by it, false teachers were on every side, and in their bosoms;—to sow tares, to pervert the mind from the simplicity of the gospel, and to strengthen prejudices not sufficiently removed. It was, therefore, necessary, that there should be faithful guides at hand to consult with, and amidst every difficulty to administer aid and consolation.

But were not the Apostles, Elders? The Apostles Peter and John expresly call themselves so: but this must, certainly, regard some *peculiarity* touching these Apostles, or as the office of apostleship, in general, led them to act on particular occasions, as pastors of distinct christian societies. However this be, it can admit of no doubt, that the Apostles, as such, were distinguished from every inferior order by this;—that they received their commission, and derived their authority, immediately from Christ himself, with original powers to teach the doctrines, and establish the laws of his spiritual kingdom.

From this idea of a christian church, a question now arises of the greatest importance upon this subject:— Whether it appears from the New Testament, that any established connection doth *now* subsist between those

primary

Chap. IV. OF THE CHURCH.

primary ministers of religion, and any subsequent order of men, whatever name they may assume: the right which the *last* holds being mediately derived from the *first*, in virtue of an original divine appointment, and a regular unbroken succession; so that those who belong to *this* order are to be properly considered as *their* successors, and vested with certain ministerial powers, which the churches or christian societies cannot confer?—Or whether the appointment of the ministers of religion doth not ultimately rest on the constitution of such christian societies, and belong to them as their exclusive right?—To arrive at some certainty in this capital point, is the design of the following chapters.

CHAP. V.

OF APOSTOLIC SUCCESSION.

SECT. I.

Of the state of the question.

THE advocates for uninterrupted succession are pleased to ask those who accuse them of holding a *lame genealogy*, to point out to them where this succession hath failed;—the age, the country, the place, the time where it hath suffered interruption? But I apprehend, nothing can be more unreasonable than such a question.—Here is a positive and bold claim to a high rank and dignity; a rank and dignity to which nothing can be produced similar in the common order of Providence; a claim to the dignity of an embassador from heaven.—Here is a claim to a sacred office upon the authority of a divine constitution and appointment, in which the whole body of Christians are not only concerned, but on which, in no small measure, their happiness as moral and accountable beings is supposed to depend: is it not agreeable to common sense, and to all our notions of common equity, that the claimants, in a case so singular and important, should fairly make out their pretensions; that they should show, that the commission, which they pretend to hold, is properly authenticated, and that the powers which they assume, are clearly included in it?—If, pretending to be the lineal

descendant

descendant of an antient and illustrious family, I claim a title to the original honours, am I to prove my right by giving a public defiance to discover any imposition, or am I to exhibit a regular succession, agreeably to the constitution of my country, terminating in my own person? Such a defiance would certainly be considered as an infallible proof of insanity. I must positively prove my propinquity to the first possessor of the honours claimed, or, at least, to one in possession of them, where the prior claim was self-evident;—and this propinquity exactly according to the succession established in the original grant. No other method could be received as a credible ground of evidence; and that for this plain reason, one may be unable to disprove an alledged fact, and yet presumptions so violent may be against it, as must greatly weaken the credit of it.—We may entertain shrewd suspicions from the nature of the fact itself, or the circumstances that attend it; so that an allegation upon general principles, without a strict and positive investigation, cannot possibly give us that satisfaction which the importance of the case may require. Perhaps this observation may seldom or never be applicable to the transmission of an estate or honours, because no one would be so wild as to give in so general and vague a claim; but it is certainly applicable in general where the interest of another is concerned, much more, where the common privileges of christianity are limited by it.

SUPPOSING, therefore, at present, that it could not be shown in what particular instances this succession hath failed, there certainly lie presumptions, from the state of primitive christianity, and the extraordinary qualifi-

cations

cations of its ministers, against the credibility of such a succession, that render this a claim highly improbable; and which, therefore, absolutely requires that these gentlemen should prove their spiritual pedigree. For who dare, in good faith, venture to affirm, that, even in the apostolic age, much more in the succeeding ages, amidst so many persecutions by which christians were scattered, or thrown into distinct societies, widely separated from one another; amidst so many prescriptions, so many migrations from one place of safety to another; amidst so many political contests and religious disputes; amidst so many divisions and contradictory opinions, that so early prevailed among christians themselves; amidst the ignorance and credulity of the multitude, and the presumption or policy of ecclesiastics;—who dare affirm with any assurance, or any probable ground of conviction, that the succession of *priests* hath been perpetuated, deriving their claims from one common apostolic source? Such a succession would, it may be maintained, have been morally impossible, without an immediate and continued interposition of divine Providence.—It would have been impossible, even, to have perpetuated and preserved pure the Jewish priesthood, where there could have been no dispute concerning the order and manner of succession, if that ecclesiastic policy had not been directed and carried forward by the peculiar superintendency and guardianship of Jehovah himself.—In order, therefore, to save this constitution from the innovations that must have been naturally introduced in the ordinary course of things, the Jews were shut out, in a great measure, from intercourse with other nations, and remained a distinct and almost an unknown people. They

were

Chap. V. OF APOSTOLIC SUCCESSION.

were hedged about with penal laws on every side, executed by God himself, as their supreme magistrate; and the nations around them were restrained and over-awed from meddling with them, except when employed as the instruments of the divine justice to punish their idolatry or disobedience. Thus their civil and ecclesiastic œconomy, but more especially the latter, was preserved from innovations of every kind, by means which no other nation ever enjoyed;—by means which christianity gives us no room to look for. We may, therefore, conclude, that no religious establishment, in the order of succession similar to this, was ever intended; because it seems self-evident, that the one could not subsist without the other.

But, not to take these pretenders to apostolic succession too short, or to seem to avoid this argument in any point of view: we return this positive answer to their question—when or where hath this succession failed? It failed, in the *primary* view, with the Apostles: it failed, in the *secondary* view, when those immediately appointed by them, or having a direct commission to appoint others were no more: because no succession can be perpetuated, but in virtue of similar powers, or some definitive law, or standing commission from those having original authority, by which this succession is ascertained, carried forward, and authenticated through every gradation of it. This proposition which, we presume, will appear to rest on the most rational principles, we shall endeavour in the sequel to illustrate and confirm.

SECT. II.

WHETHER THERE IS ANY LAW LIMITING MINISTERIAL SUCCESSION, OR EXPLAINING IN WHAT ORDER IT IS TO BE CARRIED FORWARD AND PERPETUATED.

IT hath already been observed, that the Apostles were men chosen to be witnesses for their Lord. They heard his doctrine, they saw his miracles, and conversed with him after his resurrection. And as they had uncommon means of conviction, they were endowed with uncommon powers, and had an uncommon commission to execute — to teach all nations: a commission attended with insuperable difficulties without such powers: nor have we evidence from scripture that this work was the immediate object, or peculiar province of any but those who were vested with this commission. In confirmation of this, we may further observe, that when Judas who had been numbered among the *twelve*, and had obtained a part of their ministry, had " gone to his place," they do not, in virtue of any powers they had received, presume to fill up this vacancy; but nominate two of those men " that had companied with them all the time that the Lord Jesus went out and in among them, beginning from the baptism of John unto the same day that Jesus was taken up from them, to be ordained witnesses with them of his resurrection," and appeal to heaven for a decision; " and they prayed and said, thou Lord who knowest the hearts of all men, shew whether of these men thou hast chosen, that he may take part of this ministry

nistry and apostleship, from which Judas by transgression fell; and they gave forth their lots, and the lot fell upon Matthias, and he was numbered with the Apostles." In further proof and illustration of this, we find, that Barnabas and Saul, being marked out for this office, they receive their appointment by immediate nomination from heaven, " separate me Barnabas and Saul, for the work unto which I have designed them." Thus it is evident, that the work of apostleship was not to be the effect of the most perfect human wisdom or determination. — The Apostles, therefore, neither had, nor could have had any successors by a designation of their own. They attempt no such thing, nor is any succession in this channel to be looked for.

We must direct our views, therefore, for ministerial succession to some other quarter:—Either to those who watered the vineyard, in general, and were subservient in promoting the interests of christianity, where Providence ordered their labours:—or to those to whom the oversight of certain churches were occasionally committed:—or to the fixed pastors of particular christian assemblies. Of the *first*, there were probably many distinguished with peculiar gifs and talents for public service. " To one was given the spirit of the word wisdom; to another the word of knowledge, by the same spirit; to another faith; to another the gift of healing, by the same spirit; to another the working of miracles; to another prophecy; to another discerning of spirits; to another diverse kinds of tongues; to another the interpretation of tongues." Under these are probably comprehended all that variety of gifts by which the primitive

church

church was gathered, enlarged, edified, comforted, established. But it can admit of no doubt, that they were often bestowed for special purposes, upon many who had no particular charge; and who acted sometimes as they were directed by their own wisdom and prudence, but more frequently as they were moved by the spirit.—Neither *here*, then, can we find any solid ground to rest on. These extraordinary itinerants were evidently intended as temporary ministers, and cannot stand at the head of this succession. We neither know properly the nature of their work, nor how far their commission extended.

We must, therefore, in the *next* place, inquire what information on this subject can be gathered from those who were immediately commissioned by the Apostles; and of this denomination, so far as I am able to recollect, there are only two, Timothy and Titus,—perhaps Philemon,—perhaps many more; but these two are the only persons of whom we can speak with certainty, as immediately appointed and employed for the public benefit of the churches.—And it is evident, from the accounts we have of both, that they were early companions of Paul in his travels and labours, and had never afterwards any fixed residence. We find the *one* at Ephesus, when Paul wrote his first epistle to him, and where he had formerly been with that Apostle, when he called together the elders of the church, and gave them his last affecting charge: here he remained for some time, at his request, in order to rectify certain errors, and from thence departed into Macedonia.—The *other*, at Crete, where he had come, likewise, in his travels with Paul, and where he was left for a season for important

tant purposes; but how long they respectively continued is, perhaps, uncertain. One thing is plain, that they acted as extraordinary men, by the immediate appointment, and under the immediate direction of an eminent Apostle: nor do we read of any more employed in the same work.—Without an *immediate* commission from the Apostles, or a deputation of *secondary powers* to Timothy or Titus, none could assume this office. It even seems doubtful, if any but the Apostles themselves were competent judges who were to act in this high capacity. Certainly they have committed no such secondary powers to others. There is no such thing in the New Testament as a deputation or mandate from the Apostles to Timothy or Titus to ordain colleagues in their office, and successors in *their* room, when they should be no more. I do not imagine, that there is any one who so much as pretends that there is. The office, therefore, that these two itinerant ministers held, as much ceased with primitive christianity, as the office of an Apostle.

It will be admitted, however, that with regard to the appointment of elders, or fixed pastors of particular christian assemblies, the Apostle Paul did give secondary powers. "For this cause left I thee in Crete that thou shouldest ordain Elders in every city, as I had appointed thee." Here, therefore, in the *last* place, we must direct our views for ministerial succession. On this foundation we must necessarily build the Ecclesiastic superstructure, if on any at all. But how are we to proceed in this important business? Where is the rule? where is the law immediately regarding a succes-

sion,

sion, or that can possibly direct us? we receive the Apostolic mandate with great respect, and consequently the Elders ordained by Titus as Ecclesiastics, vested with a sacred commission, and which it was unlawful for any human authority to controul; but though we are disposed to pay all due reverence to the Apostolic mandate, we can by no means agree to extend it farther than is expressed in it. This would be something worse than a mistaken compliment. It would furnish a handle for every assuming *priest* to act on a foundation, and claim an authority to which they can have no right—Paul we know, and Titus we know, and the Elders we know; *these*, though in different degrees, were distinguished by the manifestation and extraordinary gifts of the spirit: and in such hands the churches might well place unlimited confidence. But if we enquire concerning their successors, the Scripture light fails us, and we have no guide to direct our path but the usefulness and importance of the ministerial office in general—For it were in vain to urge that the precedent before us, of ordaining elders in every city, carries sufficient authority and direction in every future period of the christian church; so that the ministerial office is hereby limited to one order of men possessed of the sole powers of carrying forward this succession independent of the rights of common Christianity. The Apostolic appointment shows, indeed, the propriety of the establishment in general; that every christian society ought to have one elder or president, one of distinguished piety and prudence, to administer in the public institutions of religion, to teach and admonish in public, to advise with in private, to direct, to comfort, and in general to officiate in sacred

ered things; but it shows *not* according to what model or external form a succession of christian ministers were to be continued, *nor* confers any powers on one order of men exclusive of another. Whatever personal powers even given to Timothy or Titus of setting apart to the pastoral office, there is no general commission given, in virtue of which a succession of Ecclesiastics were to be perpetuated in a certain order, and distinguished by peculiar spiritual powers: so that, admitting while those, who were immediately appointed by the Apostles, or by others having secondary powers from them, continued in the church; admitting, even, while the ministers of religion carried their own credentials in their hands,— the divine signature appended to their commission, that the sacred office had sufficient evidence of its resting on a divine constitution, as the peculiarity of the designation, and powers suited to it; after the Apostles or others having authority from them were gone; after the ceasing of miraculous gifts, and no visible distinction subsisted between christian ministers and private christians, it is impossible to specify any law or authority by which the churches were bound; it may be affirmed with assurance that no Ecclesiastic living had a right to assume over any one society of christians, or to advance one claim, but what his capacity to edify, his superior usefulness, or the particular choice of a christian community gave him.

If it should occur to any reader in opposition to what hath been immediately advanced, " that as the ministers of religion, as far as we can observe from Scripture history, were selected by those who preceded them, that

presumption

presumption is, that things were to continue in the same train, especially as the same occasions for such ministry continued in the churches." I would beg leave to give the following answer—That were the question simply with regard to the transmission of the ministerial character, or the design of Providence in perpetuating that office in the church of Christ, the presumption from antecedent facts ought, certainly, to be sustained. But the question here, and which, to every attentive reader, will appear through the whole of this inquiry to have been in the eye of the writer, is very different—Whether it appears from the sacred record, that there is any pre-established plan for the transmission of this office; or whether a certain order of men are vested with special powers for this purpose—And, whether the office thus transmitted in the established order of succession, is accompanied with certain other powers, which can alone be conferred in this way—powers superior to the common rights of Christianity, and which neither the collective body, could it be assembled, nor any society of christians, merely as such, can possibly confer—These are the questions to which our argument immediately leads us; and where we have already in some measure supported, and will endeavour still further to support the negative. Now, in this case, where the difference between the first and succeeding ages of Christianity is so immense, where the examples insisted upon are so dissimilar to the future state Christianity—to admit of a bare presumption from precedents, would be a conception equally repugnant to all the principles of sound reasoning, and injurious to the interests of religion, the purity

purity of the faith, and that liberty with which Chrift hath made us free.

ECCLESIASTICS, no doubt, would, and actually did early assume this exclusive right of transmission, while, at the same time, they magnified certain ministerial powers which they pretended to belong to it. Here priests began this craft, which hath been more or less maintained by every denomination since their days. Nor is there a possibility of pulling them from *this* their spiritual throne, but by exposing the fallacy of this pretended chain; for while you grant the order of transmission as fixed by the divine constitution, you may be assured that every other ecclesiastic claim will infallible rise out of it — We ask, therefore, and boldly ask, where is this ecclesiastical commission from the Apostles, or from Timothy, or Titus, or even from the elders? Doth it explain the nature? Doth it direct the manner of ministerial succession? Doth it inform us who are to judge of the qualifications of ministers, by whom they are to be ordained, and to whom the right of nomination and election belongs? There is no such commission on divine record — nothing similar to it or that can be explained into a law or directory upon this subject. Nor is it necessary that there should: when it must appear to the whole world that the distinguishing work and labours of a minister in the ordinary state of christianity, required abilities only, which were to be found in every christian society — a capacity to teach, and to provide in administrating religious ordinances plain in their nature, obvious in their end, and intended for the benefit of all.— The manner, therefore, of ministerial establishment, in

the

the common order of providence, is wholly left to be determined by the circumstances, the judgment, and prudence of the churches.

This is, certainly, a conclusion to which we are necessarily led from the silence of the *new testament* upon this subject, compared with the clearness and precision which we observe in the *old* upon *one* entirely similar.—*Here* you find a priesthood by divine appointment settled into a sacred constitution and perpetuated by an order and succession obvious to all. Nothing is left to human discretion. The happiness and prosperity of a people depended upon an exact observance of their publick ritual, and therefore the laws relative to it are minutely descriptive; so that were a million selected from different countries, and of different religious sentiments, to read the description of this ecclesiastic constitution, they would all, to a tittle, agree in the same account: and can we suppose that infinite wisdom should set aside this dispensation, and introduce a new one with a succession of ministers peculiar to it, possessed of different degrees of eminence and spiritual power, and upon whose administration the happiness of no small part of his rational creation should depend, and yet that the book containing this new dispensation should not furnish us with one institute, or directory, by which we might be enabled to judge with some degree of evidence of the order of succession, or the extent of ministerial powers; that we should be left to the uncertainty and confusion of tradition, to vague conjectures, distant probabilities and precedents, and far fetched conclusions? Nothing, we apprehend, would be more inconsistent, or injurious to that wisdom
and

and goodness by which they were both framed and conducted.

SECT. III.

OF THE CAUSES THAT WOULD NATURALLY LEAD TO THIS IDEA OF APOSTOLIC SUCCESSION.

THOUGH it is sufficiently plain to every one that reads the new testament, divested of those early prejudices that bias the mind, and render it utterly incapable of every sober and rational inquiry, that there is nothing in this divine record ascertaining that particular mode of succession, by which a christian ministry is to be carried forward and perpetuated; nothing that looks like an established ecclesiastic œconomy intended as a pattern or standard for every future period, and to which we are bound to conform as a divine institute; the churches, we may readily conjecture, would be naturally led to submit to the direction of those who had been appointed by the Apostles, or those empowered by them. Let us put the case for instance, that Titus agreeably to Paul's instructions, did ordain elders in every city of Crete; though it doth not appear that these elders had any particular commission of ordaining others, we may well conclude that, when a vacancy should happen in any particular charge, or when the number of converts should encrease, and demand a new supply — no Apostle, no Titus, none having an immediate or secondary commission being present to whom they could have access: that these elders would be considered as the fittest persons for

judging

judging of the qualifications of a proper succeffor, or providing thefe new converts with a fixed paftor — probably as having an inherent right of nomination. Their own appointment by Titus without any thing further, would be judged fufficient authority, and the deftination they would make, an act fuitable to, and arifing from their office.—And it ought, in general, to be allowed, that they who had devoted their time and beft attention to the ftudy of facred things, and had been received and approved of as minifters of religion, were beft qualified to judge of the talents of thofe who were to labour in in the fame field, and to carry forward the fame work.— —But amidft the fervour of that zeal, infeparable almoft from the firft impreffions of every fpecies of religion, whether true or falfe, efpecially when the blood is warmed, and the paffions inflamed by violent oppofition, as men never fail to be partial and precipitate, the firft Chriftians would not think of diftinguifhing between a fitnefs to judge of qualifications — a power proper to be lodged in the hands of a few, and neceffary for the ends of publick edification — between this power, and a right of ordination and appointment vefted in the office : they would haftily confider both as belonging to it, and one of its effential and unalienable privileges : they would not think of marking with that attention and coolnefs, which the nature of the thing required, and to which a regard for chriftian liberty ought to have led them, the important line intended to feparate between teachers poffeffed of miraculous powers, and honoured with a divine commiffion, and others who, though they held a fimilar office, received their denomination and importance from their work and ufefulnefs. And thus, the Apoftolic

CHAP. V. OF APOSTOLIC SUCCESSION.

lic and succeeding ages would be confounded, and the same authority over the churches — the same powers of appointment and ordination supposed to belong to both — Ecclesiastics would seize and improve the opportunity, and would establish themselves into a constitution founded on precedent and traditional authority, too sacred to admit of any innovations or encroachments from the laity. And in this mannner would be laid the foundation of all that arrogance and spiritual usurpation, by which men calling themselves the embassadors of heaven, and claiming powers which God never gave, and sound policy ought to have withheld, have disgraced the religion of Christ, and exposed it to the ridicule of those who are weak enough to judge of it from the false and presumptuous claims of its ministers.

CHAP. VI.

OF ORDINATION.

SECT I.

OF THE MANNER OF DESIGNATION TO THE MINISTERIAL OFFICE UNDER THE OLD DISPENSATION.

ORDINATION is the solemn act of setting apart one for the ministerial office by prayer and laying on of hands; by which external rite the person thus set apart, among priests of every denomination, is supposed to receive certain spiritual powers characteristic of the office;—powers by which he is authorised to perform particular acts of religion, that formerly would have been not only incompetent for him, not only the highest presumption and most sacrilegious profanation, but which, without this sacred designation, would lose the whole efficacy appended to them. These offices are fewer, or more numerous, according to the different notions of ecclesiastics; but all agree in distinguishing them by one common name,—called the *Sacraments*. Now, as it is ordination, or imposition of hands, which, it is affirmed, gives validity to those ministerial acts; it is, surely, of the highest importance to Christians to arrive at some satisfaction upon a subject in which they are so highly concerned.—We shall, therefore, endeavour, with the most sacred regard to truth, so far as we can-

can discover it, to trace this point as far back as the sacred record can furnish us with any light upon it. And, in this investigation, we shall begin with laying before the candid reader the manner of appointment and designation to the priestly office, under the Jewish œconomy, that, as we proceed, he may be enabled to form a comparative view between *this* and the Christian dispensation.

NOTHING can be more pompous or solemn than the investiture into the priestly office, with which the Jewish ceremonial presents us: " Take unto thee thy brother Aaron, and his sons, that they may minister to me in the priests office:—and thou shalt make holy garments for Aaron thy brother for glory and for beauty; and these are the garments which thou shalt make (see the whole description, Lev. 28.) and thou shalt put the anointed oil upon his head, and his sons head, and shalt anoint them, that they may minister to thee in the priest's office ;—and the priest's office shall be theirs for a perpetual statute" (see further the whole ceremonial attending the inauguration, Lev. chap. 29.)—It were to no purpose to enumerate, at large, things so well known. It is sufficient to observe, that the ministers of this religion were not set apart in a single capacity, nor as distinguished with temporary powers, but as representative of a public institution:—of an order and succession of priests to be perpetuated during that dispensation. Upon this account their public installment and consecration, the sacrifices and ceremonies attending it, are no less circumstantial than singular in their nature. The family and line in which the office became hereditary, is afcertained by a public and remarkable law, precluding them from any territorial inheritance; and by another, no lefs remarkable, a proper fubfiftence is allotted for them, which, though feemingly precarious, became a facred part of their conftitution, and remained inviolable to the end of it. Hence it was impoffible for any ufurper to intrude into the priefts office, or to take this honour to himfelf, but he that was called of God, as was Aaron; fo that nothing is omitted to mark out thofe to the obfervation of every individual, whom God had chofen to officiate in holy things, and as intermediate agents between him and his people.—As a further proof of this, it is worth while to obferve, that as Aaron and his family bore but a fmall proportion to the body of the people, and the tabernacle fervice would neceffarily become too burthenfome to them; we find a folemn defignation of others to affift them in their public work. " And the Lord fpake unto Mofes faying, take the Levites from among the children of Ifrael and cleanfe them, and thus fhalt thou do unto them, &c.— and after that the Levites fhall go in to do the fervice of the tabernacle of the congregation,—for they are wholly given unto me." This order of men, though fervants and under-workers for Aaron and his fons, have their peculiar work affigned, and the precife line of diftinction drawn between them and thofe of a higher order; " Thou and thy fons fhall minifter before the tabernacle of witnefs;—they fhall keep thy charge, and the charge of the tabernacle, only they fhall not come nigh the veffels of the fanctuary and the altar, that neither you nor they alfo die." In all this there can be no difpute. The defignation, the order, the perpetuity of fucceffion,

are

are equally clear, particularly their confecration and inftallment; or the manner of appointment to their office, is defcribed and afcertained by the fame authority by which they are called to the office itfelf;—with regard to the former, the order and perpetuity of fucceffion, we have already made inquiry, and found nothing fimilar in the New Teftament; let us now fee if there is any thing in it peculiar to the ordination or public appointment of Chriftian minifters.

SECT. II.

OF THE PUBLIC DESIGNATION OF THE FIRST MINISTERS OF CHRISTIANITY.

IT may be proper to begin with obferving the manner in which the divine Author of our religion vefted the firft minifters of his fpiritual kingdom with their original commiffion.—" And when he had called the twelve, he gave them power againft unclean fpirits, and to heal all manner of difeafes; faying, go and preach, the kingdom of God is at hand." Nothing can be more fimple, and yet more grand;—more fuited to the plainnefs, and, at the fame time, the power of that religion they were to publifh to the world. Though their work was extraordinary, they are qualified for it without pomp or fhow, form or ceremony. It was intended, that the religion of Jefus fhould operate in fpirit and in power, void of every oftentatious exhibition that might gratify the fenfes, and by which religion, in every former period, through its natural tendency to divert the mind from the immediate object of worfhip, had been perverted; he, therefore, in his first commission to his disciples, gives a sample of that amiable simplicity, and internal power by which it should be distinguished.—Just before his ascension this commission is renewed and enlarged: formerly it respected only the lost sheep of the house of Israel, now it extends to all nations: but the same simplicity is observed; no external rite, no ceremony, no solemn form. "And Jesus spake unto them saying, all power is given unto you in heaven and in earth. Go ye, therefore, and teach all nations, baptizing them in the name of the Father, and of the Son, and of the Holy Ghost; and lo I am alway with you, even unto the end of the world." This is the last commission that Christ Jesus left behind him, and which may be considered as a formal designation to the work of apostleship; and as it was accompanied with nothing external, if it be taken as wholly limited to the Apostles, neither doth it suppose or authorise any, if the commission is considered as extending to every future minister of his religion.

"Our Lord, it may be argued, while bodily present, had no occasion to use any forms of admission. He could authoritatively give the blessing and efficacy: besides his church, was not yet formed into societies under different spiritual teachers and directors subjected to general laws, and directed by a particular œconomy. It was after he was gone only that it became necessary to leave some tokens of that power with which he was pleased to vest his ministers; some external symbol with which the divine efficacy was immediately connected in the stated order of providence." True, our Lord had no occasion to use any external forms, and yet we certainly know that he did, though indeed sparingly, use them. He *laid his hands* on the sick and healed them; and he made a salve of spittle and clay to anoint the eyes of one born blind, that he might receive his sight, and by this means he did receive it. He used means that had no connection with the end, that he might show his power in giving efficacy to them, as well as in producing no less extraordinary effects without them — And we may reasonably conclude, that if the validity of the ministerial function, and the efficacy of ministerial acts arising from it, had, in the constitution of his spiritual kingdom, been suspended on any external form of admission, he would have used that form in appointing and impowering the first ministers of his religion, as an authorised pattern and mode for all succeeding ones. Or, if after his departure only it became necessary to establish some sacred rite by which their admission into the ministerial office was, not only to be signified, but to be perpetuated and distinguished by a peculiar efficacy accompanying it; would it not have been expressed in the body of the original commission, or somewhere else in a plain and decisive manner by the great head and founder of the christian church? — Passing over this, however, and allowing every one to judge as he shall see more or less weight in it; we shall proceed to inquire what is to be learned with certainty concerning this rite of laying on of hands from the Apostolic writings, what precedents they furnish, and how far precedents establish a law; whether it was peculiar to the ministerial office, and appears to have been intended for perpetuity — or merely a temporary form.

SECT.

SECT. III.

WHAT PRECEDENTS THE APOSTOLIC WRITINGS FURNISH ON THIS SUBJECT.

THE zeal of the primitive christians, together with the great authority which the Apostles had acquired, as might have been naturally expected, begot an unlimited confidence in them. " For they who believed sold all that they had, and brought the money and laid it at their feet ? To make the necessary and prudent application of such great funds required no small degree of honesty, skill, and attention. It was a public trust of great concern. The twelve were otherwise employed and moved in a higher sphere. It was, therefore, by no means fit, that they " should leave the ministry of the word and serve tables." How then was this business to be conducted so as to prevent all grounds of suspicion, and render, at the same time, the public funds most beneficial ? The moneys were the gift of the christian society, and they only had a just title to chuse administrators. " Therefore they called the multitude of the disciples unto them, and said, Brethren, look ye out among you seven men of good report and full of the Holy Ghost and wisdom, whom ye may appoint over this business: and the saying pleased the whole multitude and they chose Stephen — whom they set before the Apostles, and they prayed and *laid their hands* upon them." This is the first time we read of imposition of hands; and from this example we can fetch no precedent with regard

gard either to the ministerial office, or the communication of extraordinary powers. For, in the *first* place, this was a distinguished case: the common stock of the believers lay in the Apostle's hands, to the equal distribution of which they could not attend, amidst their more important work; it became necessary, therefore, that men should be chosen, and, to give them proper authority, solemnly set apart as trustees for the public: and, however they might have employed afterwards whether in teaching or baptizing, it is evident that these were no part of their original appointment and institution. *This* simply regarded the business of the poor. They were not ordained christian ministers but treasurers of the public funds. *Secondly*, these public trustees did not receive their qualification from their ordination, not one virtue of which they were not formerly possessed; but contrary-wise they were appointed to this work, as being men of honest report, full of the Holy Ghost, and of wisdom. Their ordination, therefore, is to be considered only as a public and solemn declaration of their election. Nor doth it appear that the twelve ordained more, in this or any other capacity. Their general commission included in it, no doubt, every measure necessary for the progress of Christianity, and the edification of the churches. But what particular pastors they appointed, or with regard to what churches, we are entirely in the dark. The sacred writers furnish us with nothing on this subject to gratify our curiosity. It seems to have been no part of their design to give an account of these matters. Their great view appears evidently to have been, from a few general instances to point out to us the manner in which primitive Christianity was planted, the great

opposition

opposition it met with, and how far its influence extended; and to set an example before us of the zeal and fortitude, the unwearied labour and attention, the holiness, humility, and contempt of the world, by which its first ministers were so eminently distinguished—as a lesson of infinitely greater importance than the constitution of the most perfect hierarchy upon earth.

To those who have received their ideas, and formed their opinions on this subject from conversation with Ecclesiastics or reading their books, it will hardly appear credible that the Scriptures should be silent on this subject; and yet it is a fact indisputably certain, that there is not one act of ministerial ordination specially mentioned in the history of the Apostles, or in all the Epistles—if we except the case of Barnabas and Paul, and who it is plain were not ordained by any of the Apostles, but by men who, at that time, held the same character and rank in the churches with themselves. " Now, says the historian, there were in the church certain prophets and teachers, Barnabas, Lucius of Cyrene, Manaen and Saul, and as they ministred and fasted—the Holy Ghost said, separate me Barnabas and Saul for the work whereunto I have called them—And they fasted and prayed and *laid their hands* upon them"—What were the peculiar qualifications or office of these prophets and teachers, it is not necessary nor perhaps easy to determine—it is sufficient to observe here, that both were offices, in *order*, different from the Apostolic, and yet these teachers are authorised to ordain Barnabas and Saul, and to separate them for the work of apostleship—Barnabas and Paul being thus commissioned, seem to have

directed

directed their attention, in a particular manner, to supply the churches with fixed pastors elders in every church; but what particular forms they used, except that their public appointment was accompanied with prayer, we are not informed. " And when they had ordained them elders in every church, they commended them to the Lord"—We are left under the same uncertainty with regard to the form or order in which Titus proceeded in ordaining elders in every city of Crete; as we have nothing on record further on this subject but the end, or general purpose for which Paul left him in this island. " For this cause left I thee at Crete, that thou shouldest ordain elders in every city"—That the appointment of those primitive ministers of religion was accompanied by prayer and laying on of hands, is however, highly probable from the general admonition to Timothy; " Lay thy hands suddenly on no man," and again, " Neglect not the gift that is in thee, which was given thee by prophecy, with the laying on of the hands of the prysbetery:" and to the same purpose, " Stir up the gift that is in thee by the putting on of my hands."—From all these it may be allowed that laying on of hands was a rite commonly used in ordaining to the ministerial office—but it ought *here* to be carefully observed that there is nothing in this that renders it a rite peculiar to ministerial appointment—For it is affirmed, that extraordinary gifts were conferred *without* this rite, and that they were communicated *by* it, not merely to the first ministers of religion, but to christians in general. Now, if extraordinary and miraculous powers were not confined to it, if this rite was commonly

commonly used in conferring these extraordinary powers on christians in general, I desire to know in what respect it can possibly be considered as characteristic of the ministerial office?

WHAT we have here affirmed, and which, we apprehend, will serve to throw very considerable light upon this question, we shall now proceed to prove from the most decisive evidence. *First*, extraordinary gifts were communicated without imposition of hands. " Then Peter said unto them, repent and be baptized in the name of Christ Jesus for the remission of sins, and ye shall receive the Holy Ghost—while Peter yet spake these words the Holy Ghost fell on all them that heard the word; and they who believed were astonished for they heard them speak with tongues, and magnify God." *Secondly*, extraordinary gifts were communicated to christians in general by imposition of hands. " Now when the Apostles had heard that Samaria had received the word God, they sent unto them Peter and John, who when they were come prayed that they might receive the Holy Ghost, for as yet he had fallen upon none of them; only they believed on the Lord Jesus, then laid they *their hands upon them*, and they received the Holy Ghost." Here it is plain that their believing in the Lord Jesus is not considered as in itself sufficient for all the ends of primitive Christianity, without the falling of the Holy Ghost upon them—*as yet*, says the historian, plainly intimating that such an event was common, and to be looked for under that extraordinary dispensation. Again, " And it came to pass that Paul came to Ephesus, and finding certain disciples he

said

said unto them, have ye received the Holy Ghost since ye believed?" This question which the Apostle puts on the common faith of christians, evidently supposes that believing and receiving the Holy Ghost, were generally at this period connected together. Being informed that they had been baptized only unto John's baptism, the Apostle takes occasion from the testimony of this illustrious prophet to lead them to the knowledge of Jesus, to whom John bore so honourable record. "When they heard this, they were baptized into the name of the Lord Jesus, and when he had *laid his hands upon them*, the Holy Ghost came upon them, and they spake with tongues and prophecied."

THUS it appears, with the utmost force of evidence, that the extraordinary gifts of the Holy Ghost were conferred without imposition of hands, and that this rite was commonly used in conferring extraordinary powers on the primitive christians in general; so that neither these gifts, nor laying on of hands, were peculiar to the ministerial office.—Supposing, therefore, that by laying on of hands, whether of Barnabas or Saul, of Timothy or Titus, or the presbytery, the Holy Ghost was conferred on the first ministers of religion:—there is nothing peculiar in *this*, since others received the same gifts, and in the same manner, who are neither apostles, nor evangelists, nor elders, nor prophets, nor teachers. Supposing further, that all who were ordained to the ministerial office, were ordained by imposition of hands: neither is there any thing characteristic *here*; since it will admit of no doubt, that this was a form used in communicating gifts of the Holy Ghost on many other occasions.

occasions. We may, therefore, conclude, that there is not the least evidence in all the apostolic writings, that ordination, as implying the communication of certain spiritual gifts by imposition of hands, was a rite appropriated to the pastoral office intended to render its ministrations valid, and to distinguish ecclesiastic officers from the body of christians by certain invisible powers.

SECT. IV.

OF THE CONTINUANCE OF THIS RITE IN THE CHRISTIAN CHURCH.

THE attentive and intelligent reader will immediately perceive, that, admitting imposition of hands to have been a solemn rite, by which the first ministers of christianity were admitted to their office, there still remains a question of great importance on this subject; what evidence there is that this form of investiture was designed to be continued in the christian church? This is, certainly, a question on which we have a right to be satisfied, and where the evidence, we apprehend, must ultimately rest upon a clear proof of one of these following assertions:—That there is an express law declaring, that this is no temporary rite:—That it appears from the circumstances of the case, or from the nature of the rite itself, that it is of perpetual obligation, and to be observed in all times and places:—Or that the same, or similar effects, have attended it in every future period, that were observed to accompany it during the apostolic age.

THAT there is no express law declaring, that this is no

no temporary rite, but of perpetual obligation, the moſt zealous friends of the hierarchy muſt allow, and indeed muſt be ſelf-evident to every reader of the New Teſtament.—As to the circumſtances of the caſe, it hath been evidently ſhown, that they were peculiar and extraordinary; that as it was not uſed, ſo far as appears from the apoſtolic writers, in any common caſe, or by any ordinary perſon, neither was it limited to the ordination of miniſters. And, ſurely, there is nothing in the rite or external form itſelf, abſtractly conſidered, that hath the moſt diſtant relation to the miniſterial office, or any duty of it. It is a mere arbitrary form, and in its own nature of the ſame importance as waving your hand in the air, or putting it into your boſom. The importance of this rite, therefore, and the deſign of its continuance in the chriſtian church, muſt be determined in the *laſt* place, from the effects of it. If the ſame effects have been evidently perceived in every future age down from the apoſtolic, there can be no doubt —we have the cleareſt proof of the exiſtence of the ſame cauſe, while the ſign and the thing ſignified do accompany one another;—and here we are willing to reſt the deciſion. But eccleſiaſtics, it is to be feared, will beg to be excuſed: their pretenſions will not bear ſo equitable a trial. If prieſts have been occaſionally poſſeſſed of the knack of wonder-working, it muſt be confeſſed, they have been very ſparing of exhibitions of this ſort, where ſcience or knowledge had gained any ground;— and their wonders are now no more. The light hath at once expoſed, and baniſhed them from the greateſt part of Europe. The environs of the inquiſition, or the cells of monkiſh ſuperſtition, thoſe darkeſt abodes of

K popery,

popery, may still produce some memorable facts of this kind among its credulous and deluded votaries; but the *priesthood* are become too wise to expose their cause to the ridicule of the world by pretensions of this kind.

At the same time it ought to be admitted as a thing highly probable, that the extraordinary gifts of the Holy Ghost were continued in the christian church after the apostolic age, as circumstances and occasions required; as particular events, and the more or less settled state of the christian church, rendered the exertion of those gifts necessary. But, perhaps, it is impossible to arrive at any certainty in this matter. A spirit of party and emulation so quickly arose, the marks of bigotry, credulity, and superstition so evidently discover themselves, among writers of all denominations, in the ages even immediately succeeding the apostolic; but above all, an unhappy propensity of substituting ingenuity, or human authority, upon the ruins of genuine christianity, as render them altogether incompetent to judge, or give evidence in any one point, that might have tended to support a favourite notion, to raise or sink the credit of a party or a creed. But supposing that we could arrive at certainty, and fix with precision, how long the Holy Ghost was communicated by laying on of hands, instead of serving to prove, that this rite ought to be continued in the Christian Church as a sacred form of admission to the ministerial function, or to support the cause of apostolic succession, it would operate another way, and serve as an unanswerable argument against both. It would show, that Providence intended, that, along with these powers, the external sign or form should cease by
which

which they were communicated; and that in the ordinary course of things, the capital distinction of the ministerial office should arise from those talents and qualifications most eminently adapted to public edification. And if the choice of public teachers came at any period to depend upon these, and by these alone they were fitted for their work, what should render that rite and external sign *necessary* which added nothing? Is it possible to give a satisfying account why it should be considered as *essential* to the ministerial office, when the thing signified by it is no more;—if it be not still to impose upon the weak and superstitious some confused notions of divine communications?

This, it may be alledged, is an unfair conclusion;— and it may be argued, " that in the ceremony itself there is nothing which suggests the idea of extraordinary powers; and as some form of destination is necessary for ascertaining the ministerial office, this appears, not only innocent, but as suitable as any other.—When people are tinctured with superstition, any ceremony whatever, a touch of the hand, a word may be supposed to convey supernatural powers. Thus the words, " this is my body," pronounced by the priest, are supposed by all present to produce the most miraculous metamorphosis that can be conceived; and yet the same words spoken by a minister in a protestant congregation, no one imagines to be attended with the same effect: nor would a person argue justly who should insist, that protestants should lay them aside for fear of introducing the doctrine of transubstantiation: and is not the argument against laying on of hands the same?"

In return to this I have several things to offer, which, it is hoped, will in some measure deserve the reader's attention, and serve, still further, to elucidate this point.

In the *first* place, this objection goes entirely upon a mistake of the author's argument. He is not reasoning against *this* or *that* form of designation to the ministerial function. He admits, that all forms, as such, are equally innocent, and that some may be in their nature, or by custom, more suitable than others; and if there are any who think the form in question of this denomination, he is by no means disposed to differ from them. His reasoning is entirely levelled against this form as *necessary* and *essential* it itself; as necessary to constitute the ministerial character, as essential to the validity of ministerial acts; and, in this view, the whole of his argument points against the connection between laying on of hands, and certain spiritual powers, supposed to be communicated by this external rite. Dissolve *this* connection, in which the whole fascination of priestcraft lies; and he acknowledges, that imposition of hands is a very innocent ceremony.

He begs it may be observed, in the *second* place, that though it is true that, among people deeply tinctured with superstition, any ceremony whatever may be supposed to be connected with extraordinary powers—were it, " the driving of a nail into a door;" the question is how they come to be tinctured with this superstition which so easily connects ends and means that have no relation to one another? Is it not by a false association of ideas formed into a habit? And is not *this* owing
to

to the early impreffion of certain ecclefiaftic tenets, not only indifputable, but which it would be impious to oppofe? Why doth a popifh congregation believe that, by pronouncing thefe words " this is my body," fo miraculous a metamorphofis is produced—and why do the fame words pronounced in a proteftant one carry in them no fuch conviction? It is evidently becaufe the one from their infancy have been taught to believe fo, and would think it criminal for one moment to entertain a doubt of it; and becaufe the other have been warned againft the delufion, and have been taught to believe otherwife.—And were proteftant minifters of every denomination, as willing to fpeak out plainly, and at the fame pains to tell their people that there is no connection, in the ordinary courfe of Providence, between ordination by laying on of hands, and the communication of any powers but what were formerly beftowed by nature, grace, or education, the people would be in as little danger of miftaking in the *latter* as in the *former* cafe—That, at prefent, they labour under no fmall delufion, is evident from the fuperftitious notions that, almoft univerfally, prevail even in proteftant communities. Among many inftances that might be produced, the value they put upon the prayers of a minifter upon a death-bed, though they can neither attend to what is faid, nor feem to have had any former impreffions of religion, and the dreadful apprehenfions they entertain leaft their little ones fhould die without baptifm, are indifputable proofs. Are thefe rational convictions, or are they agreeable to any declarations in the facred writings? can rational or fcriptural religion be founded upon them? And, yet, it can admit of no doubt that

thefe,

these, and every other superstitious notion almost, derive their origin from false ideas of ecclesiastic powers.—And is it any matter of wonder, when upon inquiry it will be found, that the greater number of protestant ministers, instead of rectifying their mistakes on this subject, strenuously maintain an indissoluble connection between laying on of hands—of the bishop, or presbybetery, on some order that they hold to be of Apostolic institution, and the validity of the ministerial office; and this, not merely in point of decency and external order, but a divine institute? of what avail then is it that the ceremony is innocent in itself, and implies nothing that can convey the idea of extraordinary powers? —Things antecedently indifferent when abused as the means of superstition, and misleading the mind by false ideas, lose their nature and become real evils. And in particular if any rite or external symbol hath been accompanied with an extraordinary virtue or efficacy by the divine appointment, but which is evidently withdrawn in the order of Providecce; if it shall still remain the object of veneration and undue regard, and prove the means of misleading the mind of the weak and credulous in matters of high importance, it ought, surely, on that account to be abolished. " He did that which was right in the sight of the Lord—he removed the high places, brake the images, and cut down the groves, and brake in pieces the brazen serpent which Moses had made, for unto those days the children of Israel did burn incense unto it."

As a further proof that protestant churches entertain certain misapprehensions on this subject,—whatever may be be the opinion of individuals, who neither confider it as a ground of feparation, nor are poffeffed of influence fufficient to rectify the error—the diftinction made between a licence to preach the Gofpel, and a power to adminifter the facraments, ought not to be omitted. From whence it is afked doth this diftinction arife, and from what caufe is it juftified, if there be no powers fuppofed to be conveyed by laying on of hands, which the perfon ordained was not poffeffed of before,—if no virtue be derived from this ceremony which gives to thefe facred inftitutions their peculiar efficacy—or at leaft an efficacy which they could not poffibly have had, if difpenfed by a mere licenciate? Can fuch a diftinction fail to miflead the people, and to create thofe fuperftitious notions which we have mentioned? Is it not an *inexhauftible* fource of fuperftition, if Ecclefiaftics are difpofed to avail themfelves of it? and doth it not indicate fome capital miftake in proteftant minifters, both with regard to this admiffary rite, and thofe inftitutions of Chriftians?—If thefe queftions can admit of a rational and fatisfying reply, without juftifying the attempt that hath been made, to feparate between this rite, and thofe falfe or artificial ideas, that ignorance or policy have appended to it, fome labour and attention have been beftowed in vain.

CHAP. VII.

OF SACRAMENTS.

SECT. I.

OF THE IMPORT OF THIS WORD, AND THE PARTICULAR IDEA TO WHICH THE REASONING IN THE SEQUEL IS CONFINED.

IT will appear to the judicious reader, that the manner of reasoning which hath been adopted in the three foregoing chapters is of that sort, that the former argument seems to supersede the latter, and yet, upon more attentive examination, will be found to receive additional strength and confirmation from it.—Thus, if the account we have given of the Church of Christ is agreeable to the scriptural idea of it; if the rights of Christianity belong to Christians in general, and to every Christian society in particular met in the name and agreeably to the laws and doctrines of Christ, there can be no order or succession of Ecclesiastics possessed of exclusive powers. And, if it appear upon inquiry, that such a succession of Ecclesiastics, and such paramount powers are no where supported by the sacred record, we have additional evidence and confirmation that the whole privileges of Christianity belong to the Churches. Again, if there is no uninterrupted succession of Christian Ministers descending in a particular order, and fixed by a par-

ticular

ticular law, there can be no established rite for perpetuating this succession, nor any communications peculiar to it arising from the observance of this rite, and preserving this transmission; and, if it admit of a clear and positive proof that no such rite was ever instituted, as a rite peculiar to the designation of the ministerial office, nor any external form of admission to that function necessary to give validity to certain ministerial acts, it follows that an unbroken and uninterrupted succession of Christian Ministers cannot in itself be essential, because there is no authorised form of designation, nor any particular institute by which it is to be carried forward, and ascertained.—In like manner, if this rite, that is, ordination by laying on of hands, is no established form of designation to the ministerial office, nor authorised by any divine law; if thereby not one gift, not one virtue is communicated, which the person ordained did not possess before; if it imply no more than a publick and formal destination to the office, which external order and decency may require; we may rest upon it as a fair and natural conclusion that the positive institutions of Christianity, called sacraments, with regard to their validity and internal operation, are utterly independent of it.

We shall, nevertheless, proceed in the same manner with regard to the point before us—following thus the chain, link by link, which ecclesiastics have pretended to hang out to us, and to fasten upon it our eternal hopes; and shall inquire into the nature and efficacy of the sacraments, and to whom the dispensation of them belongs. And if, in our reasoning upon this article,

ticle, we shall appear to be more prolix than in the former chapters, we must beg the reader's excuse; as the wonderful virtues said to belong to these religious institutions, with the exclusive right of administration wholly assumed to themselves, is the mighty charm by which *priests* of every denomination have fascinated the minds of their deluded votaries, and gained an unlimited ascendance over their consciences. And we shall begin with endeavouring to fix the import of this word, and with what propriety it is used.

In its ordinary signification it seems to be derived from the Latin word *sacramentum*, which by the Romans was applied in a particular manner to the oath which soldiers took to be faithful to their general: and hence it hath been adopted by Christian Divines for Baptism and the Lord's Supper, which are supposed to be oaths *de fideli*; and, therefore, are known by the general name of the *Sacraments*, i. e. in other words, oaths of allegiance, submission, and fidelity.—But in a more general sense, the word imports whatever, in sacred things, is supposed to be deep and mysterious; and thus the vulgate frequently renders the Greek word μυσεριον by *sacramentum*; and the Church of Rome, in conformity to this idea, have encreased the number of their Sacraments to seven.—But there is still something more peculiar in the notion of Sacraments, and wherein the *essence* of them is supposed to consist; and that is the conveyance of certain spiritual virtues and blessings by the external use and application of some visible sign or symbol of divine institution.—Thus baptism is said to be " a sign of regeneration, whereby, as by an instrument,

they

they who receive baptism rightly, are grafted into the church :—the promise of the forgiveness of sins, and our adoption to be the sons of God, by the Holy Ghost, are visibly signed and sealed —That by the baptism of Jesus Christ in Jordan, the water was sanctified to the *mystical* washing away of sin." And still more explicitly :— " That baptism actually produces its whole effect in washing away original sin, and bringing the grace of sanctification into the soul, independent, even, of any positive disposition on the part of the receiver." The same or similar virtues are ascribed to the institution of our Lord's Supper from the same notion of its being a Sacrament, " the outward symbols of bread and wine are seals to every believer of all the benefits purchased by Christ."—Christ is given in this holy Sacrament for our spiritual food and sustenance, so that if by a lively faith we receive it, then we spiritually eat his flesh and drink his blood, we are one with Christ, and Christ with us."—These, so far as we have been to learn, are the common and received ideas which this word is supposed to imply; and as to the propriety of it to express those ideas, so far as it is understood, we have no intention to dispute; though, it is humbly suggested, that it would be more discreet to talk of Scripture institutions in Scripture language: we shall, therefore, make use of it, as we may have occasion, confining ourselves to those institutions called by this name among protestants, and to that notion alone which supposes that the Sacraments, in virtue of external signs, are accompanied with those efficacious and extraordinary virtues.—Blessings so great, suspended on means seemingly so inadequate, become suspicious in the moral order of Providence, awaken our

curiosity,

curiosity, and claim our strictest scrutiny; least we impose upon ourselves or our fellow-men in matters of such infinite concern. This shall be the subject, therefore, of some following sections.

SECT. II.

Of the Efficacy attending Baptism.

THE first question undoubtedly is, what is the doctrine of the New Testament on this subject? Is there any thing to be found here that can lead us to the idea of regeneration, and the washing away of original sin; or bringing the grace of justification into the soul, by the mere application of the rite appropriated to baptism, independent of any disposition of the receiver? To be able to give a satisfactory answer to this question, we shall inquire, *first*, if there is any law or mandate relative to this point; and, *secondly*, if there are any precedents that can throw light upon it.

As to the *first*, it is wisely ordered, that we have an express law or mandate to which we can appeal, and from attending to which we shall be enabled to judge with certainty; and if from thence it can be made appear by the rules of fair reasoning, or any mode of interpretation hitherto adopted, that there is any foundation for the Ecclesiastic tenet, that baptism washes away origina sin, or produces its whole effect of bringing the grace of justification unto the soul independent of any positive dispensation on the part of the receiver; we are willing to give up the whole controversy. The mandate then runs thus. "Go ye and *teach* all nations, *baptizing* them in the name of the Father, of the Son, and of the Holy Ghost, and lo I am with even you unto the end of the world." This is the only mandate on record—now let any one of common sense, and common integrity, say, if there be any thing expressed here, or that can be inferred from any word in the whole commission, that hath the most distant relation to infants, or original sin? The commission evidently connects *teaching* and *baptizing*, and makes the *one* the condition or foundation of the other—The Apostles were, by and by, to be sent forth to proselyte the nations, a most perilous and arduous work, where, to flesh and blood, insurmountable difficulties lay in the way, and which, therefore, required extraordinary powers and supports. Well, how were they to proceed? They were simply to preach the Gospel, and leave the effects to the divine blessing which was promised to attend them. Was any any form of admission into the christian church necessary? Whoever should believe the divine report they are commanded to baptize—an external rite of admission not peculiar to Christianity, not instituted but adopted by our Lord. "All Israel were baptized unto Moses in the cloud." The Jews received all their proselytes by baptism; and John baptized at Jordan, where Jesus himself, that he might fulfil all righteousness, was baptized himself in common with others. He therefore continues the same rite, and gives a new sanction to it, by establishing it as an external form of admission into the christian community—at once representative of the christian's profession, and figurative of his hopes; of the *first* by its purity; of the *last* by his being, as it were, burying and

rising

rising again. This is the very account that an Apostle gives of it, " being buried with Christ in baptism, and rising again with him through faith of the operation of God, who hath raise him again from the dead." Add to this that admission to the privileges and hopes of the Gospel, in those sacred names of the Father, Son, and Holy Ghost, by which the Deity was exhibited in a new and supernatural, and, at the same time, the most amiable character, could not fail to leave deep impressions on the minds of novitiates. This is a natural and just account of this rite, and its being established as a form of christian admission. It is a rite that, in no stage, or former period of its application, was supposed to be attended with remission of sin, or any extraordinary virtues. John " baptized in the wilderness and preached the baptism of repentance for the remission of sins;" and why should we imagine that any new efficacy was appended to it, when there is not one hint in the commission that can possibly lead us to such an idea? He who pretends to indulge his own fancy, where the thing in question is a matter of pure revelation, opens a door for vain and presumptuous conjectures without end, and without a possibility of arriving at certainty of any kind —Where revelation is decisive, it is our duty to submit. " Every thought, and every thing that exalteth itself against the knowledge of God, ought to be brought into captivity unto the obedience of Christ." But why will men frame mysteries for themselves, and endeavour to impose them upon others?—A doctrine seemingly so absurd as the washing away of sin, independent of every intellectual and moral act, and which would reduce religion to a mere machinery; a doctrine so inconsistent

with

with the nature of man, and the whole plan of God's moral government, would, surely, require to be supported by the most convincing and decisive evidence. I say inconsistent with the whole plan of God's moral government—for we may defy all the abettors of this tenet to produce any thing similar to it, so far as we are acquainted with that plan, and the manner of its procedure. In the natural government of the world, effects may be produced, and we have repeated instances in the divine record of their having been produced, independently of any disposition of the agent, and where there appears no connection between them, and the sign or immediate condition: thus was the leprosy of the Syrian cured, and thus were all the miracles wrought by Moses in Egypt produced: and in the same manner must every miracle performed by secondary agents be produced. They must depend upon the connection established by Infinite Power and Wisdom between the sign and the thing signified. It will be further acknowledged, that the Supreme Lord himself may, by a sovereign act of his grace, pardon sin, but in no instance does he it without working repentance and a change of disposition. It shall even be admitted here, for the sake of argument, that he may depute this power to those immediately commissioned by him, and directed by his unerring spirit—But he hath established, in the order of his moral government, no formal rite to which the pardon or washing away of sin is appended, independent of the disposition of the receiver. Here the end and the means are strictly connected together, and operate, not mechanically, but morally. The doctrine therefore of baptism

tism washing away original sin, is equally unscriptural and absurd.

Let us now inquire, in the *second* place, if there are any precedents in the sacred writings that throw light upon this point. The nature and extent of a law is best known from its general application to the particular subject which it regards. If the original mandate given to the Apostles, therefore, included in it moral ablution, we may certainly look for examples, as so many facts that illustrate and confirm this explication, as there is evidently nothing in the body of the mandate itself that leads to it — as its plain and natural import leads to a contrary conclusion. Is there any such particular application of this mandate? Are there any such examples to be found in the history of the Apostles, or the Apostolic writings? Not one. We read, indeed, that Lydia, when she believed, was baptized and her houshold; and that the jailor, upon his conversion, was baptized and his house: but who dare rest a particular conclusion sufficient to establish a doctrine of so interesting and extraordinary a nature, upon this generality? Who dare affirm that there were infants in either of those houses? Or supposing there had been, and that they were baptized, is there one thing concerning the efficacy of the external rite in washing away original sin, or producing its whole effect of bringing the grace of justification into the soul, independent of any disposition of the receiver? The contrary appears with sufficient evidence — When the jailor put the question, "Sirs, what shall I do to be saved?" the answer is, "Believe on the Lord Jesus Christ, and thou shalt be saved and *thy house.*" Was

the

the houſe to be ſaved through the jailors faith? no ſuch thing. Was it to be ſaved by being baptized? equally diſtant from the truth. How then were they to be ſaved? In the ſame manner, and by the ſame means that the jailor himſelf was — by believing. "When he brought them into his houſe he rejoiced *believing* in the Lord with *all his houſe.*" Thus were they ſaved, and, if infants are capable of believing, we ſhall allow that, if there were any in the houſe, they were ſaved likewiſe. In like manner, we may conclude, was the houſhold of Lydia baptized—"believing and rejoicing in the Lord."

The order of primitive Chriſtianity, beyond all doubt, was—believe and be baptized, nor is it poſſible for Eccleſiaſtics to produce one text to the contrary. "And the eunuch ſaid, here is water, what ſhould hinder me from being baptized, and Philip ſaid, if thou believeſt with thine heart thou mayeſt; and he anſwered and ſaid, I believe that Chriſt is the Son of God, and they both went down into the water, and he baptized him." —Beſides this one, there are ten examples of baptiſm on record in every one of which, believing, repenting, or the extraordinary gifts of the Holy Ghoſt expreſsly precede this external rite of admiſſion. (ſee Acts 2, 38. 8, 12. 8, 13. 9, 18. 10, 47. 16, 15. 16, 35. 18, 8. in this verſe are two inſtances 19, 5.)—The only caſe that may be thought an exception is that of the Apoſtle Paul, Acts, 9, 18; but whoever will attend impartially to the whole of it muſt be convinced that prior to his baptiſm he was a real convert. His conviction and the change of his diſpoſition appear two ways. Senſible that the voice which addreſſed him, was the voice of power and majesty, he asks, astonished and trembling, " who art thou Lord?" Being fully satisfied from the answers that it was Jesus, whom he persecuted in his church and people, he immediately puts the question " Lord, what wilt thou have me to do?" He is all submission and willing to be employed at his command. In the next place, having arrived at Damascus, he fasts and prays ; and to whom and in what view his prayers were addressed the narrative will leave us no room to doubt—Besides all this, it seems evident that he had likewise received the Holy Ghost before his baptism. " And putting his hands on him, Ananias said, brother Saul, the Lord, even Jesus who appeared unto thee in the way as thou camest, hath sent me that thou mightest receive thy sight, and be filled with the Holy Ghost"—Here we may observe that Ananias first addresses Saul as a brother which evidently implies the same common faith, nor is this appellation ever applied otherwise ; and then he lays his hands upon him, the ordinary sign of divine communications—saying, " Jesus hath sent me that thou mightest receive thy sight, and be filled with the Holy Ghost, and immediately he received his sight." Now can one believe that one part of his commission was fulfilled, and the other not? — that Saul received his sight by the hands of Ananias, but not the Holy Ghost? we cannot, without doing violence to every rule of connection and propriety by which words can be explained. But doth not the same sacred historian, when he represents the Apostle Paul himself giving an account of his own conversion before the chief captain at Jerusalem, best explain his own meaning? And is not the necessity of baptism for washing away sin there

plainly

plainly implied? " And now why tarriest thou? Arise and be baptized and wash away thy sins"—As this is a text, which by some is judged decisive in ascertaining the efficacy of baptism in washing away sin, it cannot be disagreeable to the reader, who desires to arrive at the knowledge of the truth, to know what support it gives to this doctrine.

And in the *first* place, it is allowed that the divine historian is the best interpreter of his own meaning: but in return we would ask, is the meaning of a writer best explained by one passage, or a dozen, all relating to the same subject? Is there any that has the sober use of his understanding that would in a question of any doubt, and where the sense was expressed with equal plainness and perspicuity, explain *eleven* places by *one*, rather than *one* by *eleven*? and yet this is exactly the state of the case with those who would insist upon this single passage as a proof that washing away of sin follows upon baptism. In all the texts immediately referred to, the historian describes the persons baptized as believers and converts. The evangelist declares that he only who *believes*, and is baptized shall be saved. And the same historian who puts the words in dispute into the Apostle's mouth, evidently describes him before his baptism a convert, a chosen vessel of God to bear his name before his Gentiles: and yet in opposition to all this evidence, more full perhaps than for any other article in the christian creed, they would deduce this tenet from one single expression. Nothing can be more absurd. Nothing can exhibit a clearer proof of prejudice and bigotry, or perhaps something worse.

WHAT then would you make of the words " be baptized and wash away thy sins?" I would certainly explain them in analogy to the whole tenor of Scripture on this subject. Neither in this view is the explication forced. Faith and baptism were inseparably connected in the plan of primitive christianity; the *last*, not as an instrument of pardon in itself, but as it was a proper expression and evidence of the *first*. Surrounded as the first christians were with enemies on all hands, a public profession confirmed by some external rite appears highly necessary: and what rite, as hath been shown, could be more suitable or expressive? Baptism, being thus the external sign of that faith to which the pardon of sin is so expressly and repeatedly promised, that it may be justly called the first and capital doctrine of Christianity, might, in a more general or secondary view without great impropriety, be in itself considered as the sign of this pardon or washing away of sin. Surely, there is nothing in all this contrary to the common and well understood forms of speech. But to bring the question with those, who struggle so hard for this text as decisive with regard to the efficacy of baptism, into a still narrower point of view. Let me ask if the case of Saul can have any relation to the baptism of infants, or original sin, without supposing that his original sin was washed away, and that his actual sins were left unpardoned? It surely cannot, and this is a supposition that cannot be admitted, because the text is evidently general and makes no such distinction " arise and be baptized, and wash away thy sins." Now how could his sins be washed away, while he still remained under the power of the more heinous and aggravated

guilt

guilt—the guilt of actual sins?—If it should be said that both original and actual sins were washed away, that baptism is sufficient for both these ends, and this without any positive disposition on the part of the receiver: why then, I would further ask, are not adults baptized, seeing the effects of this rite are evidently, according to this doctrine, more extensive with regard to them than with regard to infants? For, if Saul's sins were washed away by the mere application of the external rite, why may not the guilt of any other sinner be washed away, in the same manner, were he grown old and hoary headed in sin? Why not on a death bed? And this, I confess, next to extreme unction, or a plenary pardon from the holy see, would be the shortest and easiest expedient of getting to heaven, that the *priesthood* hath yet discovered.

We may, therefore, upon the whole, conclude, that nothing appears from the examples or precedents in Scripture to support the tenet,—whether of papists or protestants, that baptism washes away original guilt, and by the mere use of the external rite brings the grace of justification into the soul. I think we may say, without presuming too much, that the contrary appears with the most convincing evidence :—which is still further confirmed from the account the Apostle Peter gives of this rite, and in what manner it saves,—not by outward washing, but inward purity.—Let us attend to the whole passage, that the reader may be fully satisfied of its real meaning and import:: " The like figure whereunto (the ark) even baptism doth now also save us, not the putting away the filth of the flesh, but the answer of a good confcience, by the refurrection of Jefus Chrift." Now, wherein lies the propriety and force of this fimilitude, if it be not in Noah's faith as defcribed by another Apoftle: " by faith Noah being warned of God, prepared an ark for the faving of his houfe, by the which he condemned the world, and became heir of the righteoufnefs which is by faith." The long period in building the ark was a trial of his faith, in the threatenings denounced againft a wicked world, and in the deliverance promifed to him and his family; and, at once, by his ftability and perfeverance a confirmation of it. By means of his faith, therefore, he was faved. For if he had begun to doubt, and had thereby been difcouraged from his work, there had been no ark to fave him. Unto this, fays the Apoftle, baptifm is a like figure, as it is a public profeffion of our faith in all the promifes and threatenings of the Gofpel,—in all the bleffings of it; in the great deliverance and falvation exhibited in that covenant which was confirmed by the refurrection of Chrift. But as Noah, not only difcovered his faith by building the ark, but evidenced the moral effects of it by being a preacher of righteoufnefs, not ceafing to warn and admonifh a corrupt and infenfible generation, and doing according to all that the Lord commanded him. In like manner we muft act confiftently with the profeffion we have made in baptifm;—not fatisfying ourfelves with wafhing away the filth of the flefh, but having a good confcience correfponding to our faith.— It was not the mere building of the ark that faved Noah, it was his faith and his righteoufnefs. It is not the mere wafhing with water that faves in baptifm; it is faith and the anfwer of a good confcience. Thus we see that every text strengthens the rest, and leads to the same conclusion;—that baptism is the public profession of that faith, by the use of an external instituted rite; and accompanied with a suitable life and conversation, which saves.

There is one thing further on this article, which I would beg the reader's indulgence just to touch upon. It is the analogy between circumcision and baptism. It doth not occur to me indeed, that the Scriptures any where state a parallel between them, or deduce any conclusion from the one to illustrate the other: but, as divines have taken a conceit, that baptism under the Gospel comes in the place of circumcision under the law, and speak much of the last as the seal of the old, and still more of the first as the seal of the new covenant, in a manner frequently not easily to be understood, but which, upon the whole, seems designed to magnify the efficacy of baptism; we may shortly inquire from whence this notion of a seal hath arisen, and what it imports when applied to both.

There appears to me only one passage in the New Testament that seems to give the most distant countenance to this form of expression; " and he received the sign of circumcision, a seal of the righteousness of the faith which he had, being yet uncircumcised, that he might be the Father of all them that believe, though they be not circumcised, that righteousness might be imputed unto them also." Now, in order to understand the real import of this, let it be observed, that the Jews, from the zealous, and almost unsurmountable attachment to this rite, confidered it as conferring on them a fole and exclufive right to the divine favour, and could not think of embracing a religion that diffolved fo facred a bond. Hence arofe all their difputes about receiving the Gentile converts.—To obviate this grand objection, rectify their miftake, and reconcile their minds to the faith of the Gofpel, as utterly independent of it, the Apoftle employs almoft a whole epiftle; and here he traces this rite back to its origin, and fhows them, that Abraham's being the peculiar favourite of heaven was by no means the effect of his circumcifion, but that circumcifion itfelf was the feal of the righteoufnefs of *that* faith, by which, and not by this rite, he ftood forth the Father of all them that believe; to whom, in like manner, righteoufnefs would be imputed,—by thus walking in the fteps of Abraham.—What then are we to underftand by this faith of Abraham, which was thus fealed by circumcifion? What this faith was, we fo far learn from the fame Apoftle, "By faith Abraham, when he was called to go out into a place, which he fhould afterwards receive for an inheritance, obeyed; and he went out not knowing whither he went." But we have reafon to think, that there is more included in this faith, which was the feal of his righteoufnefs: becaufe the promife made to him, that he fhould become a great nation, and that all the families of the earth fhould be bleffed in him, was another proof of Abraham's faith, previous to his receiving the fign of circumcifion.—For God's firft appearance and call to him, "Get thee out of thy own country," was in Mefopotamia, and the promife was made to him after his removal from thence, when he dwelt in Charran, or Haram (fee Acts, chapter VII. verſe 2, 3, 4, compared with Gen. chapter 11. verſe 31.) The righteouſneſs imputed to Abraham appeared, therefore, in his faith in both caſes;—in the firſt by an unlimited ſubmiſſion, and ready obedience to the divine will;—in the laſt, by an unſhaken perſuaſion in the divine veracity and faithfulneſs, as well as in his power to accompliſh what he had promiſed:—theſe were expreſſive of a temper, and conſtituted a character of the higheſt moral rectitude. Now, ſays the Apoſtle, circumciſion was the ſeal of this faith. It was intended as a permanent teſtimony of it, and a viſible ſecurity for the fulfillment of the divine promiſe.—The concluſion muſt have been obvious to every intelligent Chriſtian to whom he addreſſed himſelf: the promiſe having been faithfully accompliſhed, that there was no further occaſion for the ſecurity. This, it is hoped, will be allowed to be a candid and juſt account of circumciſion as a ſeal of the righteouſneſs of faith.—And if baptiſm bears any analogy to this rite, it lies in this, that it is a public evidence of our faith and profeſſion, a public confirmation of all the gracious promiſes in the Goſpel, and a viſible ſecurity, that they ſhall be certainly fulfilled to all them that believe.

This rite had a further proſpect, which by no means lay in the Apoſtle's way to illuſtrate, and which we may juſt mention. It was the ſign of a temporal covenant with the children of Iſrael, deſigned to preſerve their community entire, until the promiſed ſeed ſhould come, and the promiſes and prophecies concerning this extraordinary perſonage ſhould appear exactly accompliſhed. Without this rite, therefore, there was no admiſſion as

a mema member of their common-wealth, nor any claim to the diftinguifhed advantages to be reaped under a polity where God himfelf appeared interefted by the moft fignal interpofitions of his Providence :—Accordingly it was a rite that could refpect *males* only. Thefe were the proper reprefentatives of the community, and therefore the fign or token, under *this reftriction*, was a fufficient claim, fo long as they continued obedient, to the bleffings promifed. Hence every uncircumcifed *male* child was to be cut off from the people, that the reprefentation might be compleat, and fully anfwer the terms of the covenant. Hence likewife the pofterity of the Patriarch were particularly diftinguifhed, fo that it fhould not be in their power to incorporate with the nations without a known defertion of their religion and people.

SECT. III.

WHETHER INFANTS ARE CHARGEABLE WITH GUILT.

HITHERTO we have delivered our own fentiments; but, in the queftion now before us, dare not pronounce a pofitive decifion. As writers of great candour, capacity, and learning, however, have prefumed to put an exprefs negative upon it; and as their opinion, if not contradicted by fcripture, which alone can give us any information on this point, would pull out the very foundation ftone upon which the efficacy of baptifm in wafhing away original fin, wholly refts — it would be doing injuftice to the fubject, not to lay before the impartial reader the outlines of what they have advanced

on

on this subject, leaving it to have what weight it appears to deserve.

Those who maintain the affirmative, insist on two texts of scripture, among others, which they hold decisive: " Among whom also *we all* had our conversation in times past in the *lusts* of our flesh, fulfilling the desires of the *flesh* and of the *mind*, and were by nature children of *wrath*, even as others — but God who is rich in mercy — hath quickened us together in Christ Jesus." Now from this it is argued, that by *nature* here the Apostle means to express the state in which all men are born, and consequently that all men are born under the wrath of God; and as the divine wrath is properly the exercise of his justice in the punishment of sin — that all men are born sinners. In answer to this, those who oppose the doctrine maintain, that there is no occasion for taking the word *nature* in this limited view, as it is evidently used by the same Apostle — not for the state in which one is born, but for custom, disposition, habit. " Doth not even *nature* itself teach you, that if a man have long hair it is a shame to him?" Doth not the custom or practice of the country teach you that this is a thing indecent? They say further, that taking the Apostle's words in connection, and as one part serves to explain another, it is plain that by nature he means habit, or an acquired disposition; because he speaks of himself and the Ephesians who had been converted to the faith of the gospel — not with regard to the state in which they were born, but their state previous to their conversion and being quickened in Christ Jesus — as " having their *former conversation* in the lusts of the
flesh,

in flesh, and fulfilling the desires of the flesh," which in no sense can be applicable to infants—and afterwards as *dead* in sins by a custom of sinning, which had grown into a habit, and rendered the mind insensible to every feeling. To confirm this explication, they further urge that the same Apostle considers man by nature, amidst all the disorders, and imperfections of his moral powers, still capable of great and worthy exertions. "For when the Gentiles which have not the law, do by *nature* the things contained in the law; these having not the law, are a law unto themselves, which shew the work of the *law written* in their *hearts* accusing, or else excusing one another.". Now, could they be born by *nature* sinners, and yet by *nature* do the things contained in the law? Could they do by nature the things contained in the law, could they be a law to themselves and their consciences bear witness and excuse them, while they were by nature under the wrath of God? Hence they conclude that man is not born under the wrath of God, and therefore not in a state of guilt.

There is another passage which the abettors of this tenet consider as unanswerable, and I shall take notice of the more, as from these two, one may be enabled to form a pretty exact judgment of the strength of the argument on both sides. "By one man sin entered into the world, and death by sin; so death hath passed upon all men, for that all have sinned." Now here, it is said, that the Apostle's words are too plain to be denied, and too strong in proof of the point in question to be got over. "*All have sinned.*" You must either exclude infants, therefore, from this *all*, or acknowlege that they

have

have sinned; but this cannot be done, without saying further that they are not only exempted from sin but death; for the *all*, in the one case, is of the same import with the *all* in the other—" Death hath passed upon *all* men, for that *all* have sinned." In answer to this again, it is affirmed, that the words, consistently with the design of the writer, or with themselves, cannot admit of this sense. The design of the writer, say they, is not to establish the doctrine in question, but simply to show that the consequences of the fall, sin and death, are more than balanced by the gracious plan of redemption — that as sin and death came by Adam, righteousness and life came by Jesus Christ; so that where sin had abounded grace might much more abound: nor can we with any propriety suppose that the Apostle, who established all his principles on the strongest chain of reasoning, would have left a doctrine of such infinite moment, to rest upon a single sentence in the form of an inference, which does by no means arise from any premises he had formerly laid down; nay, which is inconsistent with the immediately preceding position, " that by one man sin entered into the world." For how could sin have entered by one man, if all had sinned in that single act of one? Sin would have entered not by *one* but by *all*, and then the righteousness and life by Christ would have stood opposed, not to sin and death introduced by Adam, which, as hath been observed, is the leading purpose of the Apostle, but in opposition to sin and death introduced by all. The phrase therefore, " for that all have sinned," according to all the rules of sound reasoning, can import no more, than that all have shared of the effects, or suffered by the sin of one

man

man — by that fin which wrought death and all the evils of our nature.

To invalidate this reasoning, two objections are offered; *first*, That by this interpretation, the same thing is made the cause and effect: the effect expressed in the words is evidently, " so death hath passed upon all men ;" the cause, " for that all have sinned." Now, according to the above explication, say they, both amount precisely to the same thing — death hath passed upon all, for that all die ; where the cause of the death of all, " for that all have sinned," which the Apostle had affirmed, is plainly made an effect of that cause. In answer to this it is said, 1st. That the same thing is by no means made cause and effect: for the cause of the death of all is expressed in the beginning of the verse, and not in the conclusion : " by one man sin entered into the world, and death by sin "—What death ? Not merely the death of Adam, but the death of all his posterity ; " so death hath passed upon all." The sin of Adam is, therefore, the cause here assigned by the Apostle, and the second part of the sentence, " for that all have sinned," is merely an amplification, and proof from fact, of the truth of the first part, " that death hath passed upon all," and therefore expresses no more than that all actually die : and as a further proof of the propriety of this explication it is contended, that what is here translated, " all have sinned," ought to have been rendered, " all are become mortal" (see Dr. Taylor on this passage). But 2dly, it is affirmed, that by taking the words " for that all that have sinned" in an active sense for the cause of the effect, " so death hath passed

passed upon all men," you make the sin of *all*, the cause of the death of *all*, which is both false in itself, and contrary to the reasoning of the Apostle, that sin and death entered by one. The Apostle, therefore, must certainly mean, agreeably to all our ideas of propriety and sound reasoning, that, in consequence of Adam's sin, he became mortal; death was inflicted upon him as a judicial punishment, or became the natural consequence of his disobedience; that his posterity, therefore, by being universally subjected to death, the effect of Adam's sin, are in fact treated as if they were sinners, even those who have not sinned after the similitude of Adam's transgression. This they contend is a just and rational account of the words, and agreeable to the general tenor of Scripture; and that instead of confounding cause and effect, it makes the whole text consistent, intelligible and plain.

The *second* objection is, that the whole force of this reasoning goes upon the absurdity—that all men were present, and sinned personally in this one man, what no one was ever foolish enough to assert—an imputation of guilt being only contended for. But what say the opponets is an imputation of guilt? The consequences of guilt we understand, and acknowledge that in the natural order of Providence they may extend through successive generations, and involve the innocent as well as the guilty, but guilt which is personal, cannot possibly be transferred: for what is guilt, but the charge that lies against a moral agent, as being a sinner, or transgressor of the divine law; and he who is chargeable with sin is chargeable with the cause; or

upon

upon what is the charge laid? and if with the cause beyond all doubt with the effects: and so the conclusion would be the same,—that sin and death were the effects, not of the sin of *one* man, but of *all* men, which is a downright contradiction, by supposing that they were causes both of natural and moral effects before they were born. This, they insist, is no quirk to evade the force of an argument, but necessarily arises from the very construction of the words, as explained to support the doctrine of original guilt.

The opponents of this tenet add further, that the sciptures not only give no countenance to the doctrine of original guilt, but establish clear principles in direct opposition to it. Amongst many others they advance the following: "In those days, saith the Lord, they shall no more say the fathers have eaten sour grapes, and their children's teeth are set on edge, because every man shall die in his *own* iniquity; every man that eateth the sour grapes *his* teeth shall be set on edge." Now, say they, *those days* refer to the gospel days, as evidently appears from the subsequent verses. "Behold the days come that I will make a new covenant with the house of Israel, not according to the covenant that I made with their fathers, when I took them by the hand to bring them out of the land of Egypt," which promise they argue cannot possibly regard exemption from temporal punishment, or the consequences that arise from the order of Providence; though it is introduced in answer to a complaint of this kind: for it still holds true that children suffer in many instances on account of the folly and vices of their parents, even in a rational capacity,

capacity, though in a lesser degree: this promise must, therefore, regard the future consequences of vice, and the effects of guilt in general, as they shall appear fairly balanced in the final completion of the divine administration more fully explained in the gospel — Under which dispensation of divine grace to men, the promise gives the fullest assurance that "the son should not bear the iniquity of his father, but that the soul that sinneth shall die,"—consequently that those natural evils which arise from the order and constitution of Providence, and which may seem in the mean time inconsistent with justice, are permitted, and intended for the happiness of the sufferer, if he is not wanting to himself, and shall be fully accounted for.

Another principle, which they affirm to be established in Scripture is,—That it is a law only that can inform us of our duty, when we have transgressed, and to what punishment we stand in justice exposed; and this they confirm by the Apostolic maxim, "that where there is no law, there is no transgression."—And again, "the law worketh wrath." To suppose, therefore, wrath, or punishment, without the transgression of a law would be absurd. And will any one, add they, seriously maintain, that infants are capable of knowing or transgressing a law; or that without transgression there can be guilt?—That, if there are any such, it is impossible to argue with them on the principles of Scripture or of reason:—on the principles of Scripture, since it is here expressly asserted, that where there is no law there is no transgression: and, what is a law, but a rule of duty enforced by proper authority, fully explained and understood?

understood?—On the principles of reason; because these confirm the doctrine established in the Scriptures, and gives us the fullest assurance, on the one hand, that no creature can be the subject of a moral law who can neither understand nor obey it; and, on the other, that to suppose such a creature by the constitution of its nature subjected to final misery, is utterly inconsistent with every idea we can possibly form of the righteous Lord of the universe.—To support this argument, they reason thus:—It depended, without doubt, on the determination of the great Lord of the universe, what rank any of his creatures should hold, and, in particular, what superior advantages his rational creatures should enjoy; because *these* being the sole effect of his free bounty, he might have bestowed them with a more or less sparing hand: while existence, upon the whole, remained a blessing, there could be no cause of complaint; nothing inconsistent with our ideas of divine rectitude. He might have subjected them to death, therefore, by the original constitution of their nature, or by any other intermediate step, which to infinite wisdom should appear best; but that he should have subjected them to a state, wherein they would be exposed to all the misery consequential upon guilt, without any act of their own, or saved by a remedy entirely dependent on the pleasure of another, is impossible to suppose, without the highest indignity to the honour and rectitude of his moral government. It would be to represent him as sporting in the most cruel and tyrannical exercise of his power, and acting in opposition to his plainest and most solemn declarations. " Therefore, thou Son of Man speak unto the House of Israel, thus ye speak saying, if our transgressions

gressions and our sins be upon us, and we pine away in them, how should we then live? Say unto them, as I live saith the Lord, I have no pleasure in the death of him that dieth.—Turn ye, turn ye, why will ye die, O House of Israel?"

It is difficult, therefore, say they to determine, whether the notion of original sin, or the expedient that *priests* have contrived of washing it away, by flinging a few drops of water from their finger ends, is to be considered as the greatest reflection on the righteous Lord.

Such is the general state of the argument. If you assume the negative, you thereby supersede every dispute concerning the efficacy of baptism in washing away original sin. If you fall in with the orthodox and popular doctrine, and maintain the affirmative, the reasoning in the former section remains entire and unhurt.

SECT. IV.

Of the efficacy attending the Lord's Supper.

We now go forward to the second positive institution of Christianity, and shall examine into the particular virtues ascribed to it, formerly taken notice of (section II.) The original institution is as follows: "And he took bread, and gave thanks, and brake, and gave unto them, saying, this is my body which is given for you; do this in remembrance of me. Likewise also, after the supper the cup, saying, this cup is the New Testament in my blood shed for you; as oft as ye eat this bread, and drink this cup, ye shew forth the Lord's death until he come again." This is the institution. And taking it aside from every human commentary, could one easily be brought to think, that this were a *great mystery?* Surely there is nothing here of which the mind doth not perceive the meaning, the end, the reasonableness and propriety.—Great and distinguished events have been commemorated in all ages, and among all nations, by some action and external rite or symbol expressive of public joy and gratitude. Sacred and profane history are full of them. In conformity to these, but more especially to the *passover* instituted to preserve the remembrance of a signal deliverance, and which the Jews themselves considered as typical of *that* greater by the Messiah, when he should come in his power and glory to redeem them from all their enemies, our Lord appoints this memorial of himself, and his love to sinners in laying down his life for them, to be observed by all his friends to the end of the world. And what could be more suitable to the end he had in view?—Eating and drinking together in a social manner hath ever been esteemed a sign of friendship, and, at the same time, serves to strengthen it. Eating and drinking together in a religious view *consecrates* that friendship, and, besides, hath an immediate tendency in this institution, to impress on the mind a deep sense of the inestimable blessings of *redemption:* of that bread which came down from heaven for the life of men. By external and visible signs it brings to our imagination, more readily, the whole tragedy of our Lord's sufferings, and affects the soul more

more forcibly; thereby exciting every devout affection—particularly, humiliating views of ourselves, and the most profound admiration of the divine condescension and mercy; a holy indignation, and hearty purposes against sin, a noble elevation above the world, and love to one another. All these effects this institution is fitted to produce in a moral, gradual, and progressive manner, thus operating agreeably to its nature, and similar to every other duty of religion.—Nor doth it any where appear, that it is accompanied with effects of a more extraordinary nature; or that a divine efficacy, or divine virtues, of any kind, are communicated in any other manner.—As there are some passages of Scripture, however urged in support of those enthusiastic, and we may venture to affirm, equally unscriptural, and unintelligible notions, of " sealing to believers the benefits purchased by Christ;" " giving Christ in this Sacrament for spiritual food," and in general of God's communicating, in this ordinance, as by a vehicle, immediately and powerfully with the souls of men,—by certain manifestations, impressions, spiritual fervors, and effusions of divine grace. It may be proper to take notice of them, where we shall have occasion to lay open further the nature of this institution, and, at the same time, to show how they have been perverted and abused.

The *first* is a part of the institution itself, " This cup is the New Testament in my blood shed for you." Now, from this it is inferred, that partaking of the cup, and consequently of the bread, is the *seal* of the new covenant, or the covenant of grace, and if, of the covenant, then of all the blessings contained in it.—But why

why the feal? Do not the words themfelves exprefs their own meaning fufficiently? Certainly they do: for neither cup nor wine could, in the nature of things, be a New Teftament; for it is a New Teftament in blood. "This cup is the New Teftament in *my blood*," i. e. a new legacy of bleffings purchafed and confirmed by blood: the cup or wine, therefore, can be no more than the external fymbol of this blood. The bleffings are fealed by the blood, and the blood is reprefented by the cup, fo that in truth, if we *will* fpeak of *feals*, the bread and the wine are but the figns or fymbols of the *feals* of this New Teftament;—the bleffings of which belong to every believer,—to every friend of Chrift, who doeth whatfoever he commandeth, and, in particular, who doeth *this* in remembrance of him. It is our devout remembrance of the death of the Son of God, and the fenfe we thereby exprefs of the great bleffings we hope for by it, with the practical improvement that arifes from fuch a public and folemn profeffion of this hope, that conftitutes the very characteriftic of this divine inftitution. "For as oft as ye eat of this bread, and drink of this cup, ye fhew forth your Lord's death till he come again."—Thus it is evident, that the inftitution itfelf plainly expreffes its own meaning and end; fo that every other virtue, or efficacy appended to it, is wholly the fuperaddition of human invention.

The *second* paffage that deferves notice is, "The cup of bleffing which we blefs, is it not the communion of the blood of Chrift, and the bread which we break, is it not the communion of the body of Chrift?" which words, is it faid, are a plain declaration, that partaking

taking of the cup and the bread is a direct act of spiritual communion between Chriſt and the ſoul. And what if it ſhould? Is not every act of religious worſhip, if performed with a proper temper, an immediate act of ſpiritual communion? Is not prayer in a ſpecial manner, where, in words the moſt humble and fervent, and in poſture the moſt reverent and ſubmiſſive, we addreſs our Maker, an immediate act of ſpiritual communion? When deeply retired within himſelf, the devout worſhipper pours out his ſoul before him who knows his thoughts afar off, and who dwells with the man of a contrite ſpirit—can we ſuppoſe any intercourſe between God and the ſoul more immediate or ſpiritual? Nay, it may be ſaid with the higheſt aſſurance, that he who lives in the habitual and conſcientious diſcharge of his duty, holds daily communion with God. "If we walk in the light as he alſo is in the light, then we have communion with one another, and the blood of Chriſt cleanſeth us from all iniquity"—"If any man love me he will keep my words, and my Father will love him, and we will come into him, and make our abode with him." Not one text ſo ſtrong in all the New Teſtament is to be produced to juſtify the extravagant notions concerning the Lord's ſupper.—But, in order to underſtand the real import of theſe words, it is proper to attend to the immediate point the Apoſtle had in view; which, if any one chuſes to look at the words with attention, will evidently appear to be as follows:—Corinthians, your conduct is very inconſiſtent, and highly blameable with regard to the ſacred inſtitution of the ſupper. Is not this ſolemn rite of eating bread and drinking wine, as a memorial of the death of Chriſt, and the grand benefits purchased by it, a peculiar badge of your christian character? do ye not thereby profess to have renounced heathenism and idolatry, and to acknowledge the divine author of this institution for your Lord and Master, to submit to his authority, and to be directed by his laws? And will ye yet enter into the temples of idols, and eat things offered to them, and thereby join in communion with unconverted Gentiles in their worship of their false deities? By eating that bread which represents the body of Christ, and drinking that wine, which represents his blood, ye profess to hold communion with him, and to derive your hopes of eternal happiness from him, and will ye act a part so evidently inconsistent as likewise to hold communion with fictitious Gods, who, in truth, are devils? For, " I say that the things which the Gentiles sacrifice, they sacrifice unto devils, and I would not that ye should have fellowship with devils. Ye cannot drink of the cup of the Lord, and the cup of devils, ye cannot be partakers of the Lord's table, and of the table of devils." This is the Apostle's argument, and hath entirely a reference to the impious practice immediately taken notice of, which, it seems some professing christians were led to from their connections with the heathens, or from prejudices still remaining with regard to that worship from which they had been so lately converted.

A *third* passage is, " For he that eateth and drinketh unworthily, eateth and drinketh damnation to himself." From which it was pretended, that if the danger of communicating unworthily is so great, the advantages arising from communicating worthily must be in proportion— That worthily participating of this ordinance hath an excellent

cellent tendency to infpire pious and divine affections into the foul, and to promote the fpiritual life, and that, along with the practice of the other duties of religion, it will gradually form the mind into a heavenly temper, and thereby qualify it for future happinefs, is acknowledged: and that unworthy participating is a high act of profanation, and indicates a mind void of every fenfe of religion, is likewife admitted; but neither the one, nor the other fave or damn by themfelves; nor was it the intention of the Apoftle to affert any thing fo abfurd. He feems to have had no view to the final punifhment of wicked men, or unworthy partakers, on the one hand, nor to any peculiar benefits arifing from worthy partaking, on the other. His difcourfe refers entirely, as is almoft univerfally acknowledged, to certain prefent and temporal punifhments inflicted, immediately by the hand of God, as a vifible difplay of his difpleafure againft a grofs abufe of this inftitution, which the Corinthians were guilty of, and that in fo notorious a manner, as few, it is prefumed, are likely to be charged with—The cafe was this, under pretence of meeting to celebrate this divine fervice, they not only made no difference between it and a common meal, but behaved like riotous people in a tavern—fome of them getting drunk and reeling home from their affemblies. This was not to eat the Lord's fupper, as the Apoftle tells them: it was converting a facred duty into a drunken debauch, and expofing the chriftian character in a moft fcandalous manner: and therefore as a caution to others, and left the heathen fhould blafpheme, required fome manifeft and fignal interpofition of Providence to mark the offenders. " For this caufe many of them were weak,

and

and many were fallen afleep." They are therefore warmly admonifhed to difcern the Lord's body, that is the great end of this chriftian fervice, and that temper which alone could render it acceptable—or if they fhould engage in this folemn and facred rite in a thoughtlefs, diffipated, and licentious manner, they thereby eat and drunk damnation to themfelves—they moft affuredly expofed themfelves to the divine judgments—fevere bodily difeafes, perhaps death itfelf.

There is ftill one paffage further that merits particular attention. Romanifts triumph in it as a decifive proof of the *real* prefence—and *priefts* of every denomination as " an irrefragable evidence that fpiritual life and grace, and a right to immortality, are made to depend on a worthy participation of the *eucharift*." This noted paffage is to be found, John, Ch. 6. v. 53, 54. " Then faid Jefus unto them, verily, verily, I fay unto you, except ye eat the flefh and drink the blood of the fon of man, ye have no life in you, whofo eateth my flefh and drinketh my blood hath eternal life, and I will raife him up at the laft day." Thefe are the words, and we beg that the candid reader may follow us ftep by ftep, while we attempt to afcertain the genuine fenfe of them.

Let it be obferved then, that the immediate point between our Lord and the Jews was, concerning his divine character: believing on him as the Meffiah promifed, and confequently the evidence of his publick miffion. This will be found to be the leading queftion on all occafions between him and them. This point, in the chapter

ter now before us, was introduced by another—The people had discovered a great forwardness in following him, after having been miraculously fed with a few loaves: Jesus, who knew what was in man, immediately perceiving their false views, tells them without disguise, "Ye seek me not because ye saw the miracles, but because ye did eat of the loaves and were filled." Ye are entirely led by gross and carnal views, and do not perceive the evidence of my divine commission, though exhibited in the most satisfying manner to your senses.— Ye pursue with keenness and assiduity that bread which perisheth, overlooking altogether that which endureth unto eternal life. Hence it is evident that by the bread that perisheth our Lord refers to the loaves, and by the bread that endureth to everlasting life, to the hopes of eternal glory by him as the Messiah, and the means by which they were to obtain it—for this bread the Son of man *whom the Father had sealed* was to give. —And that the Jews, though their prejudices would not permit them to attend to the plainest and most convincing proofs of his divinity, understood him as speaking of the means of eternal happiness under the metaphor of bread, seems pretty plain, first, because they were habituated to consider the highest spiritual blessings under this idea, as appears from a maxim established among them, "Blessed is he that shall eat bread in the kingdom of God." Luke, chap. 14, 13. Secondly, from the question they immediately put to Jesus, "What shall we do that we might work the works of God?"— He had called upon them to labour for this bread that endureth unto everlasting life, and they seem to be convinced that, as it was to be obtained in no other way,

it

it well deserved their most active endeavours: What shall we do then that we might work the works of God ? What further working doth God require of us as the means of eternal happiness ? We are strict observers of the law of Moses, is any thing further necessary ? Can we perform any works greater or better, seeing he that doth these things shall live by them ? This is the plain meaning of the question, or it can have no connection with what goes before; and in this view it may be considered as a serious inquiry, or put in the way of ridicule and triumph. Jesus, however, gives a plain and decisive answer to it; " This is the work of God, that ye believe on him whom he hath sent." Ye rest your hopes of salvation on the law, and the works ye perform in obedience to it; these ye consider as your everlasting food; but I tell you that there is another work which God requires, and by which he is eminently glorified, believing on him whom he hath sent,—the promised Messiah, through whom alone you are to look for eternal life; and who now holds out to you the means that lead to it: this is the bread of which I am speaking, and " which the Son of man shall give unto you;" because for this end he was sent into the world and *sealed* — vested with a divine commission by the Father. In consequence of this plain answer, which could not be mistaken, the return made is evidently in point; " What sign showest thou that we may see and believe thee ?" Our fathers did eat manna in the wilderness, &c. verse 31, 32, Moses fed our fathers in the wilderness for the space of forty years; this was an incontestible proof of his divine mission, what dost thou work ? Jesus doth not see fit minutely to enter into the argument,

ment, and by a comparison between himself and Moses, in every point of view, to show his superior character, and that his mission was attended with superior evidence; but keeping in his eye the instance they had already specified of their having been fed with manna, he continues his similitude, only adopting the word *manna* for that of bread, as he finds occasion;—and endeavours to persuade them, that in him they had a more wonderful proof of the extraordinary interposition of Providence than their fathers had, in this very instance, through the ministry of Moses.—That the bread of which they boasted was not from heaven in the same sense, and for the same important ends, that he came from heaven;— that this manna descended from the upper regions of the air only; he from the throne of God;—that it administered for a season to a temporal life; that he was that bread of which if a man eat, he shall never die: " Verily, verily, I say unto you, Moses gave you not that bread from heaven; but my Father giveth you the true bread from heaven; for the bread of God is he that cometh down from heaven, and giveth life unto the world."—It is, therefore, self-evident, that our Lord speaks here of himself, and the great blessings of his spiritual kingdom, under the metaphor of bread; and that by eating this bread he understands believing in him is no less evident, " and Jesus said unto them, he that cometh unto me shall never hunger, and he that believeth on me shall never thirst; but I have said unto you that ye have seen me and believe not." I am the bread of which I speak, and by eating of this bread, I mean believing on me: but all the means I have hitherto used, though under the aptest similitudes I have

held

held forth the truth unto you, have been in vain.—"ye have seen me" "this living bread" "and believe not" v. 35. Can there be any doubt, after this, what our Lord intends by eating his flesh and drinking his blood? seeing his flesh and his blood were given for the life of the world, that is to obtain all those spiritual blessings necessary to our eternal happiness, and by faith in him alone these blessings can be obtained?—Or if there should remain any, the conclusion of this discourse is left on record on purpose to remove them. "It is the spirit that quickeneth, the flesh profiteth nothing, the words that I speak they are spirit and they are life." The whole strain of this discourse is to be interpreted in a spiritual sense, ye are, therefore, wholly inexcusable if ye mistake my words, or pretend to stumble, as if they carried the absurdity in them — of this man, giving his flesh to eat.

But setting aside this plain key to the words, it appears from other considerations, that they cannot possibly refer to this Christian service. It was not yet instituted, and, therefore, they to whom Christ speaks could have no notion of it, nor form any idea of his meaning; how then could they be blameable on this account;—upon what grounds could he find fault with them? Besides, the words in question are evidently an universal proposition adapted to all times and places, without exception where the religion of Christ is, or shall be known; and to the very time and circumstances in which they were spoken. Now, in the first place, if we suppose them immediately applicable to the Lord's Supper, they were by no means adapted to the circumstances of those to
whom

whom Christ addresses himself; for they were not yet believers;—and can we admit any thing so absurd, as that he should explain to unbelievers the import and peculiar virtues of a particular external rite of his religion, and which in a special manner is considered as a badge of it?—That he should charge them with ignorance and obstinacy in not understanding, or opposing a detached part of a system, while they were ignorant of, and rejected the whole?—Neither, in the second place, is it universally true, that he who hears the Gospel preached, and professes to believe it, may have access to partake of the *Eucharist*. His situation in life may render it utterly impracticable; and yet the proposition admits of no limitation; "Except ye eat the flesh of the Son of man, and drink his blood, ye have no life in you." They must, therefore, admit of a sense applicable to every situation in which the Christian can be placed:—add to this, that there is an efficacy ascribed to this eating and drinking, which the wildest enthusiast, or the most furious bigot, will not pretend to ascribe to the act of communicating, "whoso eateth my flesh, and drinketh my blood, hath *eternal life*, and I will raise him up at the last day." Hold, you go too far. Most assuredly he who partakes *worthily* shall have eternal life—What do you mean by partaking *worthily?* Is it partaking with proper dispositions of soul, faith, love, godly sorrow? No doubt; these are characteristics of a good man, and a good man shall certainly be saved by *this* along with the other means of religion. But will any one be foolish, or presumptuous enough to assert that the simple act of eating and drinking saves? This eating and drinking, therefore, must, in the very

nature

nature of it, refer to something, to which, agreeably to the whole tenor of Scripture, *eternal life* is absolutely promised: and *that* is faith in Jesus Christ the Son of God, the Saviour of the word.

In opposition to this it is said, that this interpretation makes flesh and blood signify the doctrine of Christ, which cannot be, seeing it is expressly said, "That the bread that I will give is my flesh, which I will give for the life of the world:" but Christ's doctrine was not offered up for the life of the world, but his flesh and his blood only." True, the doctrine of Christ was not offered up: no one ever thought of asserting a thing so senseless. But is it not *the capital* and distinguishing doctrine of Christianity, that Christ was offered up to bear the sins of many—and that he actually bore our sins on his own body on the tree? May not faith in this proposition, therefore, with the doctrines, precepts, and institutes inseparably connected with it, and resting upon it as their foundation, with the greatest propriety stand for the whole system of his religion? And doth it not precisely amount to the same thing, whether we say we are saved by the doctrine of Christ, or by Christ dying, seeing his sufferings and death signified by giving his flesh, is the great object of the christian's faith, and the primary doctrine of his religion? How pitiful is it then, to quibble about words, and to pretend to avail one's self of difference of sounds when the sense is obviously the same? Nothing can be more unworthy of the candour or dignity of a reasoner.—We may, upon the whole, therefore, pronounce with the utmost assurance that this noted passage can have no relation to this institution.

It may be thought, that there is an evident mark of diſtinction put upon this ordinance, by the particular revelation made concerning it to the Apoſtle Paul. But there can be no weight in this: becauſe not merely with regard to this inſtitution but the whole ſyſtem of chriſtianity, the Apoſtle was inſtructed by immediate revelation. "I certify unto you, brethren, that the Goſpel which was preached of me was not after man: for I neither received it of man, nor was I taught it but by the revelation of Jeſus Chriſt. For when it pleaſed God to reveal his Son in me, I went not up to Jeruſalem, I conferred not with fleſh and blood—Now the thing that I write unto you, before God I lie not." This inſtitution, therefore, ſtands exactly on the ſame foot, as to the Apoſtle's knowledge of it, with the other parts of Chriſtianity.

SECT. V.

OF THE RIGHT OF DISPENSING THE POSITIVE INSTITUTIONS OF CHRISTIANITY.

AN important branch of this inquiry ſtill remains, and that is,—ſuppoſing for argument's ſake, that *theſe* inſtitutions are attended with all the extraordinary virtues that *prieſtcraft* or enthùſiaſm have aſcribed to them—To whom doth the diſpenſation of them properly belong? Are they a part of the common rights of Chriſtianity, or are they committed into the hands of a certain order of men, who have the ſole and excluſive right of adminiſtrating them? Muſt the body of christians receive them from *their* hands, or *lose* the benefit of them? If the sacraments are really what ecclesiastics of every denomination almost, would make them, and come up to the idea we have given of them from their own words. (Sect. 2d.) This is surely a question of the greatest moment. It is a question whether the great blessings which the Gospel exhibits, and renders necessary to our Salvation, are left open to every individual, or are converted into a mere monopoly. The liberty with which Christ hath made us free depends on the answer.—And though, from what hath been already offered, it appears with the clearest evidence; that whatever privileges belong to the church of Christ, belong to the body of christians in general, and to every particular society met in his name and agreeable to his laws; that the notion of Apostolic succession, and the mysterious chain established by *laying on of hands* is entirely without foundation; and that what are called the sacraments are possessed of no special efficacy by any immediate divine appointment or promise, as distinguished from the other parts of religion—In order, if possible, to lay the ax to the root of the tree, and strike at every pillar on which Ecclesiastic usurpation stands; we shall *now* endeavour to show, that no order of priests have any exclusive right of administration, but that *these* institutions are a part of the common privileges of Christianity.—To begin with baptism.

AND here we are sufficiently sensible, that the whole church of Rome expresly deny the necessity of a priest to administer, and even anathematize those who affirm the contrary; and so far they are consistent with themselves,

selves, while they affirm that the mere application of the external rite washes away original sin, and brings the grace of justification into the soul; neither have the church of England expressly asserted that it is necessary, though it can admit of no doubt, that the sentiments of the original compilers of their service, at baptism, point evidently this way. What length the church of Scotland have gone on this head, will be best seen from their public confession—And in general it is well known that the whole body of *nonjurors*, and *high flyers* of every denomination, agree in maintaining the necessity of *priestly* ordination to give validity to this institution. This point, notwithstanding those who hold the negative, appears, therefore, to merit particular attention.

THE first sermon that the apostle Peter preached had the happy effect of converting three thousand souls. There were but twelve apostles, Matthias included; and and we have no reason to think that the one hundred and twenty that composed the infant-church were vested with any specific commission. The original form of baptism was immersion, or dipping in water, whence the Apostle Paul calls it, " being buried with Christ in baptism."—Now can any one, in his sober senses, imagine that the twelve Apostles went to work, and with their own hands immersed three thousand? Allowing an equal share to every Apostle, two hundred and fifty;— this had been a huge task. Is it reasonable, therefore, to suppose, that the new converts performed the work themselves under the eye of the Apostles, or that the whole church assisted in this ceremony. And very becoming

coming it was, in such circumstances, that they who themselves were already initiated into the Christian faith, should assist in receiving their new proselyted brethren, under this, or any other instituted form, as an evidence of their common profession: and that they were all baptized we cannot doubt, the historian expresly informing us, "that they who gladly heard the word were baptized;" and which must necessarily refer to the three thousand immediately mentioned, for we read of no more who believed at this time. Besides, there is no instance of believing without baptism immediately following upon it.

Soon after Peter and John, having wrought a notable miracle, we are informed that five thousand more believed. Who were to perform the office of baptism? Peter and John? Impossible; and we have no authority to conclude, that any more of the Apostolic class were present; for only Peter and John went up into the temple to pray. But supposing the twelve at hand, were they equal to the mighty labour of plunging five thousand? It is by no means credible. Add to this, that the present circumstances were very unfavourable for such a work.—A council of priests being instantly assembled full of deadly rage against Peter and John, and concerting how they might destroy them; and which, by the way, furnishes another presumptive argument, that the other Apostles were not present, or they would doubtless have been involved in the common plan of destruction; and yet they do not appear before the council, nor are their names so much as mentioned. We may certainly

certainly conclude, therefore, that these five thousand were not baptized by the hands of the Apostles.

To remove this difficulty, it may possibly be alleged, that the seventy sent by our Lord himself upon an extraordinary embassy, and who probably were of the hundred and twenty that assembled at Jerusalem after his resurrection, assisted at this work. To this it may be answered, that mere conjecturing is by no means to be admitted in a case that requires positive evidence;—*perhaps* they assisted,—*perhaps* they did not. Both are equally satisfactory, if we could affirm nothing further. But to throw the weight on the negative side. It ought to be observed, that, besides their not being once mentioned by the writer of the apostolic acts, we know nothing about the duration of their commission. It is just narrated by Luke, without further notice being taken of them, or, of it, so that we cannot even pretend to say, that they acted in their extraordinary capacity, during all the time of our Lord's abode upon earth.—The contrary, at least, is probable, and that their commission, which seems to have been intended to make way for his reception, and was certainly limited to the Jewish nation, was temporary only. The twelve had a similar commission, but it did not constitute their apostolic character. It was necessary, therefore, that they should receive a new embassy to teach and baptize, and the seventy not being included in this last and characteristic commission, gives us the highest presumption, if not the most satisfying evidence, that they were not designed for the same public work.

In further confirmation, that the dispensation of this ordinance doth not depend on *priestly* ordination, let it be observed, that when Peter was called to attend Cornelius, the Roman Centurion,—in expectation of the Apostle, to whom, admonished by a vision, he had sent a special message; the good man had brought together a goodly number of his friends. Peter arrives, is gladly received, preaches Jesus, and " the Holy Ghost fell on them that heard the word." Well, " can any one forbid that these should be baptized?" No, surely. But who is to perform the office, and administer the *sacrament* of baptism? Who, but Peter? No such thing. The venerable Apostle had not yet it seems, laid the foundation of his future *church*, or been so well acquainted with the secret of the *keys* as his successors. " And he commanded them to be baptized in the name of the Lord." But on whom could he lay his commands? doubtless on " those of the circumcision who believed"— a few private christians who were distinguished by no ecclesiastic commission: for there was neither Apostle nor Elder with him.

The Apostle Paul himself was baptized by a private disciple: " And there was a certain *disciple* at Damascus named *Ananias*, and to him said the Lord, arise and go—call for Saul of Tarsus, and he entered the house and put his hands upon him, and he received his sight, and arose and was baptized." But Ananias, it will be said, had a special commission, and that God may employ what instruments he pleases in carrying forward his own ends. So he may, and so he doth. But let it be observed, never in opposition to his own established and declared

declared plan. He might have employed any tribe in Israel as well as that of Levi, to have ministred to him in holy things. They had no natural or preferable right. The difference rested alone on the divine determination: but after that tribe was particularly marked out for the sacred office, and the divine commission extended, we do not observe that infinite wisdom recedes in one step from it—The application is obvious with regard to the point in view. If the Apostles or those authorised by them, had been the only persons empowered in the New Testament-Œconomy to baptize, this would have been a declared limitation of that right to a certain Ecclesiastic order; and it would have been a plain recession from the divine institution to have employed a private disciple in this sacred department—a thing that ought not to be supposed, or admitted, but where the same end would not have been answered by the established plan of Providence, which cannot be pretended in the present case: because it is evident that the circumstances of Paul's conversion might have been so ordered as to have brought him with equal advantage under the immediate care of an Apostle, or some one holding a ministerial commission in the stated order of succession; or one of this class might have been appointed to attend this extraordinary convert. The employing of a private disciple, therefore, if it was not intended on purpose, plainly shows that no general plan was established, by which this rite was confined to any order of men by a divine law.

If from all this it is not self evident that the validity of baptism doth not depend on ordination, or any mode of ministerial succession, it appears, at least, with such probability, as will satisfy every candid inquirer—where things are left so much in general, without any definitive law, or fixed rule to which we can appeal; and, certainly, ought to make those who differ in opinion very modest in their decisions.

WHY then, it will be said, did Christ himself give a particular commission to the Apostles to baptize—a special commission seems to be without any meaning if it is not limited to the persons mentioned in it? To this the answer appears by no means difficult. The commission to the Apostles is not properly a commission empowering them to baptize. This is not intended as the *speciality* of it. Baptism had been immemorially practised among the Jews as a rite of admission to all their proselytes. There was, therefore, nothing peculiar here as the object of a new commission, this rite being a mere transference of an external mode from the Jewish to the Christian Church.—The great design of the apostolic commission evidently regards the singular work in which they were to be engaged—of witnessing for their Lord, and preaching his gospel to all nations: a work to which no human power were equal. It required a special call, and special assistance. *This* call, and the *assurance* of *this* assistance, are surely the substance and strength of the apostolic commission. True, they were likewise to baptize under new names expressive of the plan of redemption, and of the faith and hope of Christians. But there was nothing in this that required an extraordinary commission: nothing but what any one might perform. Not so—to preach the gospel in spirit and in power;

to

to rife fuperior to the opinion, the principles, the fear of the world, to endure all things for the fake of Chrift, and not to " count their life too dear fo they might fulfil the miniftry they had received of the Lord Jefus." Hence the Apoftles every where fpeak of preaching the Gofpel as their great work, and what fpecially diftinguifhed their commiffion: " It is not reafon that we fhould leave the word of God, we will give ourfelves continually to the *miniftry* of the *word*;" by which is certainly to be underftood, preaching the Gofpel, as is evident from the application of this phrafe the *word* through the whole New Teftament — excepting where it is applied to Chrift himfelf the divine author of it. In conformity to this account, the Apoftle Paul tells us that Chrift fent him not to baptize, but to preach the Gofpel, and that he baptized only Crifpus and Gaius, with the houfhold of Stephanus. " Befides, I know not if I baptized any other." Nor in any of his Epiftles, while he infifts at large on the duties of the minifterial office, doth he once mention baptifm as a part of this work — Can any one then permit himfelf to think, that the fame ideas were entertained of this rite in the Apoftolic age, that have fince been adopted and propagated by Ecclefiaftics?

We now go on to inquire how far the Holy Supper is the common privilege of Chriftianity.

Though the twelve were only prefent with our Lord when this chriftian fervice was inftituted, it feems evident from the nature of it, that they reprefented every future fociety, and that it was defigned as the common duty

duty and privelege of christians. There is not one insinuation of a power of dispensing it peculiar to *them* as ecclesiastic officers. It was an action to be performed by his disciples and followers in remembrance of him, until he should come again, and that without exception of persons, time, or place. The Apostles had not at the first celebration received their commission in that character. It is plain they were not yet fitted for it. " And I brought him unto thy disciples, and they could not cure him." They did not yet believe that Christ was to rise again. " But we trusted it had been he who should have redeemed Israel." Their faith was limited and extremely imperfect. In the character, therefore of private disciples they partook of the supper, and as a pattern to others.

In confirmation of this, it is to be particularly attended to—first—That their Apostolic commission doth not once mention this institution as any part of it, or in the remotest degree as belonging to the Apostolic office—secondly—That, when the Apostle Paul delivers this institution to the Corinthians by immediate revelation, as a law to which they were to appeal, and a rule by which afterwads, in their christian assemblies, they were to be directed, he takes notice neither of the manner, nor powers of administration, but plainly speaks of it as the common and indispensible duty of all christians—If there had been any peculiarity attending this institution —if it had been unlawful to receive the symbols of bread and wine, but from the hand of an Apostle, or one deriving powers in the order of Apostolic succession; it is wonderful, that neither the institution itself, the original

nal Apoſtolic mandate, nor Paul's delivery to the church of Corinth on this head, ſhould take any notice of it — By what authority, therefore, if in neither of theſe, nor in any other part of ſcripture, there is any limitation mentioned, or any appropriation in virtue of original powers, or ſubſequent ſucceſſion, to eccleſiaſtics — by what authority have they arrogated this privilege to themſelves, ſo as to render it unlawful for a ſociety of chriſtians, agreeably to the laws of decency and order, to celebrate this memorial? If they have any ſuch authority let them produce it. We diſpute not, that the firſt miniſters of religion did preſide in this ſervice. But the queſtion is whether it would have been competent, — where they neither were, nor could be preſent, — for a ſociety of chriſtians aſſembled for the purpoſes of public devotion and worſhip, to read the ſcriptures, to pray, to praiſe, to have empowered one of their own number to adminiſtrate this inſtitution, or any other public ſervice in religion — one diſtinguiſhed by natural abilities and chriſtian gifts? I maintain the affirmative, and would be glad to be informed upon what principles of ſcripture or reaſon it can be re-argued.

It cannot be affirmed, I imagine, with any plauſibility, that the firſt Chriſtians were never in this ſituation, or that Chriſtians may not at any time be reduced to it. Before we read of the appointment of one beſides the Apoſtles, the church had encreaſed to twelve thouſand one hundred and twenty ſouls, who were, no doubt, divided into many different aſſemblies, and little ſocieties, frequently far ſeparated from one another, and

with

with whom the Apostles could hold no personal communion.

There were at Jerusalem, who heard Peter's sermon on the day of Penticost, an immense concourse from different and distant parts of the world; and it would appear from the narrative, that the three thousand who believed chiefly consisted of these; many of whom, we may well suppose, would after the feast, return to their own country. Were they to be deprived of the advantage of celebrating the memorial of their Saviour's dying love? Or did they carry ecclesiastic officers with them to their several abodes?—But setting aside every other consideration, it is well known that persecution quickly arose. In every quarter christians had enemies who were spies upon their conduct. Saul watched all their motions with the eye of an active and bloody persecutor, and had a signed commission from the high priest, " to bring all bound to Jerusalem in *that* way whether men or women." In such circumstances, obliged to fly for their safety, their societies must have been very private, and widely dispersed. " They were all scattered abroad, says the historian, throughout the regions of Judea and Samaria, *except the Apostles.*" Shall we conclude then, that the whole body of christians lived in the total neglect of this institution? This reasoning is still further supported from the rapid progress of the Gospel, after the conversion of the Apostle Paul, by whose ministry, in a special manner, it was spread over Greece and lesser Asia; so that you could hardly find a corner where christian societies were not formed. Who can imagine that all these could have access to an apostle, or stated minister nifter of apoftolic appointment among them. "And upon the firft day of the week, when the difciples came together to break bread, Paul preached unto them, ready to depart on the morrow." This is evidently mentioned as this ordinary and ftated meeting, and not occafioned by Paul's being with them; it was on the firft day of the week. It was to break bread—the day univerfally devoted to religious duties—a practice uniformly obferved on that day.

Did not Barnabas and Paul " ordain them elders in every church;"—and did they not make a wide circuit from their fetting out from Antioch in Syria, to their return thither again? That they ordained elders in every church, the hiftorian informs us; but whoever will attend to the preceeding and fubfequent narrative muft certainly fee, that he by no means intends to affirm, that they ordained elders in every Chriftian fociety refiding in the refpective places through which they paffed. It feems evident, that this ordination extended only to Derbe, Lyftra, Iconium, and Antioch in Pifidia. It may be, no doubt, probably concluded, that the fame reafons that induced them to fettle ftated minifters in thofe places, would led them to do fo in others. But fuppofing that they did, two things deferve attention: that prior to the appointment of Barnabas and Paul, or their progrefs from Antioch, there were Chriftians in the different cities, as well as at Antioch, who met together on the firft day of the week; that the journeying of Paul in company with Barnabas, was but a fmall part of his travels. In all *thefe* he found Chriftians, the number of which, by his zeal, knowlege, and boldnefs,

he

he greatly encreafed, but we do not read of his fixing elders among them. It is probable that their particular fituation did not yet admit of it;—but whether he did or not is wholly immaterial in this queftion; as it feems evident, beyond contradiction, from what hath been obferved, that, from the early number of converts from different and diftant parts, and the difperfion occafioned by a perfecution fhortly after the Apoftles had opened their commiffion, the primitive Chriftians, in many inftances, muft have been left to fettle an order and œconomy among themfelves for the difpenfing of this inftitution, and regulating every other Chriftian fervice. It hath, in the former chapter, been obferved, that befides the Apoftles, and thofe immediately employed by them, there were other extraordinary inftruments engaged for edifying the body of Chriftians. But as we cannot certainly define the extent of their powers or authority, it would be unreafonable to fuppofe, that every Chriftian fociety was furnifhed with one of thefe as a minifter, teacher, or prefident. It could not have been. *Their* work was not ftationary.—There would have been in this cafe no occafion at all for the ordination of elders, or the further appointment of any Ecclefiaftic officer, by Apoftolic authority. We may therefore conclude, on all the principles of probability, that the firft Chriftians did meet together in their religious affemblies, and perform this, and every other public office, in virtue of delegated powers of their own;—powers belonging to the Church of Chrift, and transferable according to the neceffity and circumftances of the cafe.

LET us now confider this point in another view, and make

make the appeal to the candid and rational Christian— And, first, let me ask from whence arises the obligation to the observance of this institution? The answer can admit of no doubt — from the authority of the command — from gratitude. And can any one bring himself to believe, that what I am commanded to do, in virtue of the highest authority; and what I am called upon to do, in point of gratitude, — that what is made my own personal act — an act expressive of certain dutiful and pious affections, can possibly be restricted to the intermediate offices, or instrumentality of others, who act by powers which I can neither give nor take away? If this carry not an absurdity in the face of it, there is no such thing to be found.———Again, I would ask what is the plain design of this institution? The answer is equally plain; " As oft as ye eat this bread, and drink this cup, ye do shew forth the Lord's death till he come " — The Lord's death, why? Because hereby Christians profess to believe that deliverance from the power of death, pardon of sin, peace with God, grace here, and glory hereafter were purchased. Now if these great and inestimable blessings are open to all; if all are importunately called upon to come and share in them; who on earth hath any right to seclude me from the memorial of them? Is the memorial more sacred than the things remembered? If the humble penitent come sensible of his misery, and eagerly desiring the blessings of the Gospel, he shall not be rejected, he shall not be sent away empty. " If any man thirst, let him come to me and drink, and him that cometh unto me I will in no wise cast out " — Nor has he the least need for this purpose to apply to any *priest* on earth, whether supreme or subordinate.

subordinate. The door of mercy stands open, and there is an "High Priest of our profession who hath passed into the heavens, and there lives to make intercession — so that if any man sin, there is an Advocate with God the Father." And this Advocate is the *friend* of man, " touched with a fellow-feeling of our infirmities;" and shall it be unlawful for him to eat bread and drink wine with a chearful heart, sanctified by a deep sense of religion, and a grateful remembrance of this Divine Benefactor through whom he hath access to God? Is he judged worthy to be admitted to the greater, and shall he be denied the less? Can he approach the dread tribunal with humble boldness, " drawing nigh in the full assurance of faith;" and shall it depend on the pleasure of a man like himself whether he shall approach the table of the Lord, and do this in remembrance of him who hath laid the foundation of this " hope towards God?" Still more: is this Christian service " a seal to every believer of all the benefits purchased by Christ to his special nourishment and growth in grace?" Is Christ given in this holy sacrament for our spiritual food and sustenance? Do we thereby dwell in Christ, and Christ in us, and shall the external administration be limited to a certain order of men, without whose intermediate offices I can have no right to partake? These are questions on the principles of Christianity and common sense, that, one would be apt to think, carry their own negative in them.

SECT.

SECT. VI.

OF THE CONSECRATION OF THE ELEMENTS.

IN the Levitical service, Consecration regarded persons, things, and places; and it is sufficiently known what were the forms peculiar to each of these. The same practice obtained among the heathen nations, accompanied, with the wildest superstition, and the most ridiculous ceremonies: an instance of which we have in the consecration of Nebuchadnezzar's golden image—Similar to these, and no less ridiculous, are the numerous consecrations still observed by the church of Rome, so formed to beget that superstitious reverence, and timid submission necessary to maintain her ecclesiastic policy—Unluckily, however, the New Testament furnishes not one example of this kind. Every species of external pageantry is utterly inconsistent with the simplicity and spirituality of its worship. " The words that I speak unto you, they are spirit, and they are life." Holiness is *here* disengaged from every thing foreign and adventitious. It *consecrates* soul and body for the service of God—a living sacrifice.

As an exception to this general assertion, it will, no doubt, be said that Christ, by blessing the bread and wine before partaking, consecrated them in the most solemn manner; and as from this idea, and the ordinary forms of consecration of the external symbols, is to be derived in a great measure those confused notions concerning

cerning myſtery, and immediate communications, that are thought to diſtinguiſh this from every other duty of religion, it is of ſome importance to explain, and ſet this matter in its genuine point of light.

The form of expreſſion, "Jeſus took the bread and bleſſed it" is only uſed by Matthew and Mark, which they too vary with regard to the cup: in the place of "bleſſed it" ſubſtituting the words "gave thanks:" and both Luke and Paul adopt this laſt form. Whatever, therefore, is the plain and genuine meaning of *giving thanks*, the ſame in all good conſtruction, muſt be the ſenſe of *bleſſing*. Now with regard to the firſt, the circumſtances of the caſe will determine with ſufficient clearneſs. "With deſire, ſaid our Lord, have I deſired to eat this paſſover:" why ſo vehemently deſire to partake of this feaſt? becauſe it was the paſſover immediately to precede, and, as it were, the prologue to his ſufferings and death—thoſe ſufferings, and that death which were to procure life and happineſs to guilty men: prompted, therefore, by the moſt ardent and generous love, he looks paſſionately forward to this event; and having now finiſhed this laſt ſupper, he takes the cup of thankſgiving into his hands, according to the manner of the Jews at the cloſe of their paſſover, and pronounces over it a ſhort and ſolemn prayer; in which, it is probable, he did not differ from their uſual and ſtated form—And now having bread and wine before him, apt repreſentations of his body which was to be broken, and of his blood which was to be ſhed; he again took the cup, and having again given thanks — no doubt ſuitably to the deſign that lay before him in
fulfilling

fulfilling the great purpose of eternal love, he gave them to his disciples as a memorial of that love—a memorial of that passover of which the former was but a type, and by which it was to be for ever superseded.

This is a plain account of our Lord's *blessing* or *giving thanks* both as it regards the passover, and the institution of the supper: for it evidently appears from the evangelist Luke that there were two thanksgivings, the one relative to the former, the other to the latter. If any thing further is intended by our Lord's blessing or giving thanks—a positive distinguishing blessing accompanying the act of communicating, it extends equally to ministers and people. It doth not depend upon any administrator. It is a blessing already obtained, and shall be most assuredly conferred on every sincere and devout communicant—Where our gracious Lord hath made no limitation, where he hath left the blessings of his Gospel free from every restraint, it is the highest presumption and impiety in poor mortals, to pretend to assume exclusive privileges, and to narrow the path.

SECT. VII.

THE DOCTRINE OF PROTESTANTS ON THIS SUBJECT NOT MISREPRESENTED.

IT will, no doubt, be objected to the reasoning in the former pages, that it unavoidably leads the reader to conclude, that it is the doctrine of protestants—

that

that the efficacy of this sacrament depends on the administrator: and this, it will be said is a gross misrepresentation. That this doctrine is no where maintained, and publickly avowed by protestants, is acknowledged; but, at the same time, it is true, that, however forward they may be in reprobating the doctrines and tenets of popery, in many instances, and in this among others, they are careful to retain what is most dangerous and alarming in the spirit of it—a dominion over the consciences of men. For, while they have been very liberal in ascribing extraordinary virtues to this ordinance, they have taken the exclusive right of dispensing it into their own hands—not in point of public order, or in virtue of any powers derived from the christian society, but as constituting an order possessed of peculiar powers, and independent of their choice. And where lies the mighty difference to a private christian, whether the efficacy depends on the *priest*, or whether this sacred rite cannot be administred without him? —If there are in nature certain medicines for the cure of particular diseases, what doth it avail the patient, if they are committed into the hands of an order of licentiates, who are entrusted with exclusive powers of dispensing them —whether the virtues reside in the medicines, or in the licentiates, since they can have no access to the one without the other? The patient may die as certainly by the inattention or obstinacy of the licentiate as if no such remedies existed—What signifies it to me, that there are certain spiritual medicines, called sacraments, possessed of extraordinary virtues in curing the diseases of the soul, if by the divine appointment, I can have no access to them but through the hands of a popish, or

protestant

proteſtant prieſt—whether they reſide in the prieſt or in the ſacrament?—If I am ready to periſh for hunger, my life depends upon the man who gives, or with-holds from me a morſel of bread; and yet in one ſenſe, it may be ſaid, that the morſel of bread, not the man, ſaves my life; that the want of it kills me, not his inhumanity: but who in his wits would be ſatisfied with ſuch a wretched diſtinction? And yet the diſtinction between the virtues reſiding in the prieſt, and in the ſacraments appears to me, not to be more ſolid or juſt, while proteſtants are diſpoſed to allow to eccleſiaſtics the excluſive claim of diſpenſing them, and, at the ſame time, the neceſſity and efficacy of them: becauſe they certainly thereby admit that they are as neceſſary as the ſacraments themſelves: and he is a ſhameful rogue of a prieſt that would deſire more.

SECT. VIII.

OF THE ABSURD CONSEQUENCES ARISING FROM THE CLAIMS OF ECCLESIASTICS.

THOUGH, in the courſe of this argument, we have been neceſſarily led to bring under the eye of the reader, more than once, ſome conſequences that unavoidably ariſe from the ſyſtem of *prieſtcraft*; it may now be proper to trace *theſe* more at large, and on more general principles.

Now there is not one principle aſcertained by a more fixed and unerring ſtandard than this:—that whatever is

neceſſary

necessary and essential to all, as moral and religious beings, ought to be common to all: because to suppose that necessary to my happiness which is not in my own power, or wholly depends on the good pleasure of another, over whom I have no authority, and concerning whose intentions or dispositions I can have no security, is to suppose a constitution the most foolish and ill natured, utterly inconsistent with our ideas of a wise and good agent. Every religious system, therefore, that leads to this conclusion is absurd.—And yet such is the system of *priestly* policy we have been endeavouring to overturn. For if what are called the Sacraments are necessary to salvation, and yet the dispensation of them is really entrusted into the hands of others, and lies at their discretion, my salvation is thereby suspended on a condition independent of my choice, or any possible exertion of my moral or intellectual powers, and this without any check or controul.—For let us suppose this notion of the indissoluble connection between Sacraments and a *certain* order of *priests* universally to obtain, and at the same time that these heavenly trustees should at any time take it into their heads—not to dispense these *seals* of the covenant of grace: who, I desire to know, has a right to compel them? Whom can you figure to yourself bold enough to assume an authority over men holding a divine commission with the keys of heaven and hell in their hands? The most powerful secular on earth, believing, in good earnest, the pretension of these venerable men to be well founded, would tremble for himself, and be disposed to pay humble homage, and unlimited submission to them —Besides, supposing a superior tribunal to which you could appeal, how should every

private

private Christian have access to it, so as to state his complaint and order his cause? Or, if he should, how would this mend the matter? You cannot, without impiety, suppose this supreme court, to which you appeal, to consist of laymen.—Embassadors of heaven subjected to the jurisdiction of common law, with regard to the exertion of their own powers;—horrid! This would be mingling heaven and earth together, and confounding every sacred distinction.—And is it possible to bring yourself to think, that a court of *priests*, who had nothing to fear from any other quarter, would condemn a brother on your account;—whose very pretensions to think and complain would appear a greater enormity, and more threatening to the common cause, than any thing that an Ecclesiastic could commit.

This may be thought undistinguishingly uncharitable;—but let the reader recollect that I am talking of mere *priests*, and then let him say, from fact and experience, in circumstances that have approached nearest to those we have supposed, whether the general tenor of the craft hath greatly contradicted any thing here insinuated? That there have been, and may be exceptions; and that Ecclesiastics who have maintained the same general principles have complained of their brethren, and would have been disposed, by their natural temper, to pursue more gentle and lenient measures, is not denied. The leading tenets of *priests* may be received, by education, as first principles; and, where there is no disposition to prompt inquiry, nor vigour of understanding to enable one to correct them,—may lodge in the same breast with soft affections and candour of soul. But this is far from being the general case: for, from whatever peculiar prejudices, or circumstances of education, the first principles may be imbibed, they are nourished by a pride and haughtiness of soul, equally jealous of an inquiry that would lessen the importance of the character, and impatient of opposition. This observation is so much justified by fact, that whatever principles of humanity, benevolence, or even friendship, a *priest* may seem to possess in common with other men, or however calm and dispassionate he may appear to be, the moment you touch the *shiboleth* of the craft, you perceive the cloud on his brow, and the storm gathering, which, if you are imprudent or obstinate enough to persist, will overtake you, and if you do not make a seasonable submission, most assuredly destroy you.

But still it may be said, that all this is merely chimerical; for how can any one be led to suppose, that men possessed of such powers, would deny the just and lawful exercise of them?—We are fully persuaded, that, if there were any truly possessed of such powers; any real embassadors of heaven living upon earth, and delegated to act in the name, and by the authority of the Almighty—they could not. But we must reason from experience, not from a fictitious, but a real character; what those assuming the character of embassadors from heaven have done, and consequently what they may do in similar circumstances. Have they not laid the most powerful Princes in Christendom;—have they not laid whole kingdoms under a spiritual interdict; and have they not extorted the most ignominious and humiliating concessions from the kings of the earth, in order to be

restored

restored again to the immunities and privileges of the church? History is full of examples of this kind, which clearly demonstrate the genius of Ecclesiastic government, where it hath been at liberty to exert itself without controul — and what a timid pitiful creature man is under the influence of superstition and *priestcraft*. But had experience brought in a more favourable report than in fact it hath done, it is still to be remembered, that power never fails to bring along with it a strong temptation to abuse it, and therefore ought never to be trusted with mortals without some certain remedy in the case of the violent and outrageous abuse of it;—perhaps after every expedient that can possibly be devised, it will be found, that nothing can prove an absolute security for the righteous and moderate use of power, but unerring wisdom and goodness alone.—But the most dangerous of all power, is a power in religion, because it is capable of the greatest perversion, and is attended with the most fatal consequences.—Civil power hath sometimes been used with moderation, where it hath been restrained by no law; and a political constitution may be so balanced, as to preserve, in equal scales, the powers of the legislator and the privileges of the people. But a power in the hands of the Ecclesiastics is incapable of this equilibrium: it will always preponderate to *their* side, until it leave nothing on the other but a mere form. Nor is it difficult to account for this difference.—A power in religion, so far as it is supposed to extend, is truly a power from God.—A power from God naturally overawes the conscience, and renders an appeal to every other tribunal impossible; and thus our understandings are abused, our moral powers are rendered incapable of

every

every exertion, and a door is opened for every impofition.

Admitting, however, at prefent, that we could depend on thefe ghoftly fathers, and reft fully affured of their confcientious difcharge of this important truft, there are certain circumftances, wherein it would be impoffible to have accefs to one of thefe apoftolic minifters. This is no trifling confideration. Let us fee then how the cafe may ftand.

The Chriftian Religion is not a mere local inftitution like the Jewifh, or carried on in a fimilar manner, under an immediate and extraordinary difpenfation of Providence. The external conftitution of the Chriftian Church refts on the fame bottom with the conftitution of civil government, and muft neceffarily fhare in the common fate of ftates and nations. A Chriftian country may be now happy in the fmiles of a zealous orthodox prince, or fupreme magiftrate, and may be nourifhed under the wings of the *Hierarchy*; fo that " they fhall fit every man under his own fig-tree, and none fhall make them afraid,"—with one of thefe *keepers* of the *feals* at his elbow. But alas, human affairs are fluctuating. This promifing and delightful fcene of church glory may darken in a moment. Some mighty unforefeen caufes may combine; the happy ftate may be thrown into convulfions, and out of the alarming ferment a revolution may break forth. A heretical prince may mount the throne, who will not permit one *prieft* to lodge within his dominions. The *fucceffors* of the Apoftles may be hunted from one lurking place to another. They may be be subjected to the most severe penal laws as deceivers of the people, and enemies to the sacred and civil rights of mankind. The people themselves may be laid under a civil interdict from holding communication with them. They may be all banished, as the Jesuits have been, as the disturbers of the peace of kingdoms;—not one *divine legate* may remain to dispense the Sacraments. A most wretched condition this!—And yet we can figure another as bad. A number of private Christians, suppose in their migration to America, are thrown upon a desolate island, or among Barbarians who never heard of so wonderful a character as a divine embassador; it is a thousand to one if these unhappy men have been so prudent as to carry a son of Levi with them; likely enough it was impossible.—There is no remedy, the order of Providence must take place. They have neither bishop nor presbyter among them; they are undone. Sad indeed! But stay; perhaps they have been lucky enough to carry their bibles with them. It signifies not a rush. Is it not the original charter? True; but it is a charter without a seal. It cannot help them. They must perish with the book of God in their hands.

"But these and all such cases, are cases of necessity, and great allowances ought to be made—so great that the most bigotted *priest* dare not pronounce a decision." This will certainly be pleaded to elude consequences necessarily resulting from the geneneral doctrine of priests and sacraments; but how justly, merits some consideration—And, in the *first* place, it is asked by what authority are these allowances fairly stated and determined? For if the same authority by which the efficacy of the sacraments

sacraments themselves, and the exclusive right of administring them is ascertained, doth not likewise state and determine those cases of necessity, the necessity becomes absolute. The fixed order of grace admits of no limitation. Let us take an example or two. "Without faith it is impossible to please God." "Repent and be converted that your sins may be blotted out." "Follow—holiness without which no man shall see the Lord." These are unconditional propositions, whether on the system of natural or revealed religion, without regard to time, place, or circumstance: they may, therefore be called necessary to Salvation. "But they are in every ones power, which is not the case in those instances you have so carefully marked." True, and this very consideration demonstrates the absurdity of maintaining that the canonical administration of sacraments is necessary to Salvation: for what is not in a christian's power at all times, and in all places, cannot be necessary to Salvation. It may be useful, it may be desirable, but it cannot be necessary. But *secondly*, the question is not concerning allowances or abatements in cases of necessity, but how the want of the sacraments shall be supplied? How shall original sin be washed away? Where are my seals of the covenant of grace? What shall I do thus deprived of my spiritual food? These are desperate spiritual wants; they must be supplied or I perish.—It is foolish, therefore, to speak of making allowances; for either some provision must be made by another channel, or the effects must take place in the established order of things: that is, original sin must remain unwashed away.—I must be left destitute of spiritual food—I can receive no seal of the covenant—I cannot eat the

flesh,

flesh, nor drink the blood of the Son of God, which alone can give a right to immortality. It is the fame thing to me as if there had never been a covenant. "Hold, we do not pretend to limit the uncovenanted mercies of God." If it pleafe your *reverences*, how far do thefe uncovenanted mercies extend? Do they actually comprehend our cafe? For if you can affure us of this, we are by no means difpofed to difpute about words. "We cannot tell, but we can promife you nothing further." Good fouls, we are mightily obliged to you for this difcovery, that inftead of being pofitively damned, we are only out of the way of falvation.— But permit us, if you pleafe, to expoftulate a little further, and to bring this matter nearer to a point if poffible. Is not this covenant, of which you fpeak, the declaration of the divine mercy, and the fecurity on which it ftands? And is not this mercy declared in a way moft fuitable to the divine perfections and the ftate of the finner? It cannot be denied. Then the whole fecret is out; where this covenant is declared, the bleffings of it cannot be conferred in another way;—and what the plain import of this is, I forbear mentioning:—"tell it not in Gath, publifh it not in the ftreets of Afkelon".

ANOTHER huge difficulty arifes from this fyftem of prieftcraft, and that is, by what infallible marks a private Chriftian is to come at the knowledge of the truth, and to arrive at entire fatisfaction amidft contending parties.—One order of priefts tells him, that there can be no church without a vifible head, the fountain of Ecclefiaftic power and authority.—That this authority was originally committed by Chrift to Peter, who again delegated

legated this spiritual jurisdiction to the *Pope* of Rome, and his *successors* in office; and who, in their turn, parcel it out at pleasure, to different orders of Ecclesiastics. Therefore, that the Church of Rome is the only true Church, that every society on earth cut off from her communion calling themselves a Church, and every one calling himself an Ecclesiastic belonging to it, — are schismatics, and *damned* heretics.——Another order, in return to this civility, pay the former the compliment of acknowledging, that the *Church* of Rome is a true Church, because she hath preserved Apostolic succession, and consequently the validity of the Sacraments; that they hold from her their ordination, and all their ministerial powers; but that being infected with many gross errors, a reformation, and separation from her, became necessary; that this reformation proceeded exactly on the plan of the Scriptures and primitive Christianity.— Agreeably to which there is an Ecclesiastic polity established, of which Bishops are the highest in order, deriving their powers as successors of the Apostles;—the inferior order deriving their ministerial authority from them; that without this order, and this communication of ministerial powers, there can be no Church;—therefore, that those calling themselves Presbyterian or Independent Churches, being without Apostolic ordination, are without mission, without authority, without order, without Sacraments.—A third roundly affirms, that whether Pope or Bishop, it is of small importance, seeing both are equally usurpers upon God's heritage, and the hierarchy, under every form, the *Whore* of *Babylon*— the *Antichrist*—the *man* of *sin*, who shall come with all deceivableness of unrighteousness; therefore, that Ecclesiastic

clesiastic government by Presbyters is the true Apostolic form, and founded upon the purity of the primitive Church.

Now, how is a plain christian to come at the bottom of these differing pretensions? He has only one way in which he can possibly satisfy his mind — that the religion of Christ cannot rest upon so doubtful and precarious a bottom.—We will even suppose that the scriptures had been more explicit, and had established a fixed order of priesthood vested with all the powers which the most ambitious ecclesiastic can pretend to, would this have wholly cleared up the difficulty and enabled any sensible inquirer to judge with certainty? The contrary is the fact. We should again be involved in a labyrinth from which it would be impossible for the greatest part of christians to extricate themselves. It is now near eighteen hundred years since this order and succession is supposed first to have taken place: and who will pretend to say that, amidst so many revolutions of nations, so many political schemes, so many impositions of designing men, such imperfect, and even contradictory accounts, he could trace this succession through all its branches, so as to pronounce with assurance that this sacred chain hath not been broken, and usurpations made on the original establishment. It may be said, that it would have been impossible to have preserved such a chain without frequent and extraordinary interpositions of Providence. We may even defy all the priests on earth to produce evidence sufficient to satisfy the judicious inquirer in what manner, by what mission, authority, or call, the first churches were furnished with pastors — and if they could

trace

trace them one by one, and say who ordained this bishop or presbyter, and who ordained that, and by what authority a third was set a part to the ministerial function, and so through the immense extent of the whole, it would be impossible to proceed downward with any certainty; the investigation would, in the most favourable point of view be extremely difficult, and the conclusion doubtful.

Such are the consequences that would necessarily arise from the chain of apostolic succession which ecclesiastics have pretended to establish — equally presumptuous in itself, injurious to the moral character of the Deity, and inconsistent with the spirit of genuine Christianity.

CHAP. VIII.

Of CHURCH DISCIPLINE.

SECT I.

What the general idea imports.

As every one hath a right to inquire and judge personally, where the subject regards religion only; no national plan can be established that binds individuals, without a manifest encroachment on that freedom of sentiment which is essential to the very being of it. If, under pretence of this freedom, any one shall assume a right to act in opposition to those laws or forms of political government, by which the undisturbed exercise of religion itself is protected, he becomes amenable to the public tribunal as a disorderly subject, and a rebel to the state; the laws he transgresses being civil laws, formed and carried into execution without regard to religious differences of any kind.—But though the very being of religion depends upon freedom of inquiry, and a liberty of serving God agreeably to the dictates of conscience; it will always be found, amidst the utmost variety of opinions that can possibly happen, that a similarity will so far prevail, as will unite men into societies agreeing in common sentiments, and one common mode of worship (see chap. III. sect. 5.)—But neither those sentiments,

timents, nor this form, fall properly under the idea of Church Discipline; because, independently of these, which are supposed to constitute their religious creed, the government of the society will require the exercise of certain laws necessary for preserving the external decencies, and the internal and moral order of it. This is the *discipline* of that society; and the exercise of it belongs to the society as such,—to one or more authorised by them to discharge this part of the public trust.

Now, these laws may derive their authority from distinct sources, both binding on the society from obligations corresponding to this authority.—The society, if not restrained by, or in opposition to any divine law, in virtue of their own intrinsic powers, may agree upon what regulations may appear most subservient to their own ideas of order and decency; and such regulations with regard to the members personally agreeing, or that shall afterwards join the society, are properly to be considered as terms of communion without submission to, or observance of which, they cannot enjoy the privileges of the society.—But whatever regulations prudence, or a regard to the external decencies of religion may dictate; if it shall appear from the word of God, that there are any laws, rules, or directions that respect Christians in general;—that respect the external or internal order to be observed in their religious assemblies, these, undoubtedly are universally binding, and claim the first regard. They do not exclude other regulations, but no human œconomy can supersede the sacred observance of them. It may be worth while, therefore, to inquire if there are any such regulations in the New Testament,

what

what they are, and what is their nature or import? This is the more necessary, as Ecclesiastics, if I am not mistaken, have assumed a power *here* likewise, which by no means belongs to them.

SECT. V.

OF THE SCRIPTURAL RULES ON THIS SUBJECT.

WHAT was the *Godly* discipline established, in what is called the primitive church, or to what *pennance those convicted of notorious crimes were put*, is of no importance in this question; because it seems to admit of little doubt, that in this, as well as in matters of greater importance, the primitive church assumed to themselves powers and authority no where supported by the unerring standard. We shall, therefore, here, as in the preceeding chapters, be directed wholly by the light of Scripture.

THE general rule of Scripture then is;—" Let all things be done decently and in order," which general rule immediately refers to an abuse among the Corinthians,—of speaking in their public assemblies in an unknown language, and that indiscriminately, so that " every one had a psalm, a doctrine, a tongue, a revelation." This had introduced great confusion among them, and had laid the foundation of just offence and ridicule, " if there come in those that are unlearned, or unbelievers, will they not say that ye are mad?" " Let all things be done therefore for edification :" and again,

"Let all things be done decently and in order." This is the special application of the general rule by the Apostle himself; though it no doubt applies to every similar case, and, in particular, hath the force of a standing law against speaking in an unknown tongue, or performing, at the same time, separate duties in religious assemblies.

Besides this general rule, there are some directions for public admonition and censure no less general, "Wherefore rebuke them sharply, that they may be sound in the faith." "Them that sin rebuke before all, that others may fear." From these it is sufficiently plain, that public reproof is the indispensible duty of the ministers of religion, in cases where any of the members of the society, in which he presides, have been guilty of sins notoriously inconsistent with their profession.—By the laws of Christianity, such members are as much subjected to open rebuke, as by the laws of civil government the transgressors of them are subjected to the penalty annexed; and if such offenders shall refuse to submit, or shall persist in their enormities, they are to be rejected, or cut off from the communion of the society. This is agreeable to all the rules of decency and moral order, and particularly supported by the divine law, "but if he refuse to hear the Church, let him be to thee as a heathen man and a publican." "A man that is a heretic after the first and second admonition reject, knowing, he that is such is subverted, and sins, being condemned of himself."—A heretic, in the Apostolic sense, is an obstinate sinner, whom neither private nor public admonition can reclaim. He is one who acts

in

in opposition to the dictates of his conscience. He is self-condemned without profiting by his convictions; and therefore ought to be publicly condemned, and dismembered from the society of which he hath rendered himself so unworthy.—Being an heretic may likewise include in it " making shipwreck concerning the faith;" maintaining and propagating errors subversive of the very foundations of Christianity;—" denying the Lord that bought them," which another Apostle calls damned heresy; or, saying with Hymeneus and Philetus, " that the resurrection is already past." But whether *these*, or other tenets are heretical, in a more general sense, *that* may be called heresy, with regard to any particular Christian society, which appears to them inconsistent with the purity of the faith, and the fundamental articles of their union: and, therefore, every such society is authorised to admonish, or reject, whatever member or members shall maintain doctrines in opposition to those fundamental articles;—but they have no authority to proceed one step further. No pains, no penalties, lie within their jurisdiction; nor are such offenders accountable to any civil tribunal, but so far only as they have been guilty of vices, or have propagated errors hurtful to good government, and the security of the commonwealth.—That alliance between the *Church* and the State is the most dangerous of all unions, where there is an established connection between heresy and certain penal laws, and where the *Church* judges in the first place of the heresy, and then commits the offender to the civil magistrate for execution. This hath been one of the most dreadful political measures of the *Church* of Rome,

P 3   equally

equally injurious to the rights of private judgment and good policy.—Few will think it worth their while to inquire, and fewer will have resolution to expose the errors of an established system where opposition and the stake are convertible terms.—The state, under the delusion of maintaining its own authority, destroys its most valuable subjects, and is the mere tool of Ecclesiastic tyranny.

It may be thought that the apostolic injunction to the church at Corinth seems evidently to carry this matter higher. " For I verily as absent in body, but present in spirit have judged already as though present concerning him that hath done this deed; in the name of the Lord Jesus, when ye are assembled together and my spirit, with the power of the Lord Jesus, to deliver such a man to satan for the destruction of the flesh, that the spirit may be saved in the day of the Lord Jesus"—especially as it is clearly confirmed by the Apostle's own practice, " of whom is Hymenœus and Alexander whom I have delivered over to Satan, that they might not blaspheme." But how far doth the apostolic injunction, or his own sentence carry this point? " From this double authority the church is certainly vested with a power, not only of rejecting scandalous offenders, whether in practice or doctrine, but imposing certain pennances upon them for the destruction of the flesh." By no means.—Let us candidly weigh the import of the passage.

In the *first* place this sentence—" delivering to Satan for the destruction of the flesh," is evidently of an extraordinary

ordinary nature. It carried its own execution in it, in the immediate infliction of certain bodily diseases designed by Providence, in the infancy of Christianity,—as a visible declaration of the divine displeasure against notorious offenders, as a confirmation of the authority of the apostolic decisions, agreeable to the promise, "whatever ye bind in earth shall be bound in heaven," and as a proof and standing warning to others in every similar case. The same order of Providence is evident in the punishment of those who had been guilty of a scandalous abuse in partaking of the Lord's Supper. "For this cause many are weak and sickly among you, and many are fallen asleep." Besides, this sentence plainly supposes, in the very nature of it, a power over Satan, and of employing him as an instrument of punishment. It cannot, therefore be considered as a law to be observed, or a precedent to be followed in the ordinary course of discipline in the church of Christ. This is further confirmed from the following considerations—In the case before us there is an immediate interposition of the apostolic authority: though absent in body, he was present in spirit. The sentence was denounced as if personally present, and from his own mouth. "When ye are gathered together and my spirit—deliver such a one to Satan." It was therefore an immediate apostolic action, and not a stated censure in virtue of any general rule or law—Because the crime of the offender was of a heinous and similar nature, He had his father's wife, a thing not named among the Gentiles—Should the same authority be pretended to, the very exercise of it would infallibly expose the presumption of the claim: no exclesiastic, nor order of ecclesiastic being possessed of a power of employing Satan as an instrument of punishment—It must be acknowleged, however, to their honour, that they have never been wanting in expedients. If their power over Satan hath ceased, they have seldom failed, where another power was fairly lodged in ther hands, to employ his visible agents in the *humane* office of destroying the flesh to save the spirit.

Upon the whole, it seems sufficiently clear from the New Testament, that the exercise of church discipline includes in it, and *only* includes in it such regulations as regard the decencies of religion—the public admonishing once and again of offenders—and on their remaining obstinate, rejecting them. Every thing beyond this is ecclesiastic tyranny.

CHAP.

CHAP. IX.

OF ABSOLUTION.

SECT. I.

OF THIS CLAIM IN GENERAL.

IT would appear from the general notions, that men entertain of pardon, that they consider it as a mere arbitrary exercise of divine mercy. But such an idea is utterly inconsistent with the nature of God as the moral governour, and the righteous Lord of the universe. Whatever God doth, he doth freely, but yet by an invariable law, which it would be as absurd to suppose him to transgress, as to cease to be. This law is the perfection and rectitude of his nature, by which he is so uniformly determined, that could we see the whole extent of his natural and moral government, it would appear one continued display of it—Forgiveness of sin, therefore, must include in it, not merely remitting the offence, and absolution from punishment, but a change in the temper and disposition of the offender; and this not merely subsequent, but antecedent to the act of forgiveness. In the order of Providence, something must pass in the mind that indicates a new temper, or otherwise forgiveness would be the mere arbitrary exercise

cife of power. To suppose that God should pardon one obstinately and wilfully continuing in sin, would be to suppose him not only acting in opposition to his moral nature, but dispensing this privilege in vain; because without a change in the mind of the person pardoned, he would nevertheless remain incapable of happiness—Hence the Gospel makes faith the absolute pre-requisite to this gracious dispensation: as thereby the soul discovers a deep sense of its unworthiness, a hearty sorrow for sin, and an unlimited submission to the terms of the Gospel—Hence likewise it is evident that God only can forgive sins: it being impossible that any created being should be acquainted with the inward dispositions of the human heart, or know its thoughts afar off.

Of all the extravagant and impious claims, therefore, which *priests* have made this of forgiving sins is the most astonishing: and yet such is the weakness and credulity of the human mind—and so effectually doth superstition destroy all its rational powers, that this doctrine was tamely received over the greatest part of Europe for many centuries; and in the darkest regions of popery, where the light of liberal inquiry hath not yet penetrated the gloom, is still believed—and perhaps, among the more ignorant and superstitious of that religion, in every country. At least I have never known any of that class, who did not appear to lay great weight upon confession and absolution. And is it wonderful that they should, who have drawn all their notions from their breviary and manuals, and who have so often experienced a false peace of conscience from the supposed exercise of a power, er, which they have been accustomed to consider as one of the sacred privileges of the Holy order?

But though this charge falls chiefly upon the Church of Rome, it is a question whether protestant churches are wholly exempted from it.—For what account can be given of any form of absolution whatever, which implies nothing on the part of him who pronounces it, or on the part of him that receives it? How should such an unmeaning form have entered into the head of any society on earth? It must certainly, therefore, have been intended in some important point of view, but which I confess is difficult to be perceived, if the idea of pardon is not appended to it. For as a solemn declaration of the pardon promised in the gospel to all that repent and believe, it can signify nothing. No one who thinks at all can be so weak as to be deceived by this account. Is the declaration of a priest more satisfying, or doth it carry more authority in it than the declaration of Christ and his Apostles? Was this declaration published in the gospel of peace that all might take the benefit of it, and be encouraged by it; or was it left to the church, that the priesthood for the peculiar honour of their office, might have the privilege of announcing the joyful tidings? What will not these men assume to themselves?— " This is running away with declamation — protestant divines assume no commission, no authoritative powers of pardoning sin." I know many of them do not: but that such a power hath been assumed, and is still assumed is certain; or why is it publickly affirmed " That Christ Jesus hath left power to his Church to absolve all sinners who truly repent and believe." If there be nothing here

here further intended than the simple declaration of the gospel, why is it said to be a power left to the church? And why doth the priest add " by *his* authority committed to me, I absolve thee from all thy sins?" In the general commission said to be given by Christ Jesus to the Church the proper limitation is added " who truly repent and believe," but in the particular application by the priest to the person absolved, there is no such limitation — he is *simpliciter* absolved from all his sins. This limitation, it will be said, is understood, and I will not pretend to say it is not: but I appeal to every man of sense and candour, who is acquainted with the superstition that prevails among the lower class, if there be not something *here*, that must unavoidably lead such to think, that this is an authoritative deed accompanied with some peculiar efficacy, as distinguished from the declarations of pardon in the gospel to sinners in general. For my own part I confess I never could perceive the meaning of this form, as a part of a public religious office; and would be glad to see it explained upon rational, protestant, and christian principles. The claim of the Romanists is known: they speak out plainly: but, while protestants profess to reject this claim, why should they retain, and seem to put a distinguished value upon any form in their religious service that leaves ground for the most distant suspicions against themselves? It may not be unacceptable, perhaps, to some readers to examine shortly into the foundations of this claim as it regards the Church of Rome: if there are any similar pretensions, they must stand or fall together.

SECT.

SECT. II.

CONCERNING THE FOUNDATION ON WHICH THIS CLAIM RESTS.

HOW far, on particular occasions and for wise and important reasons, God may see fit to discover the hidden things, even of the hearts of other men; or how far he may communicate to men such a power over life and death, as he did with regard to both in the case of Ananias and Saphira, we do not pretend to determine. But a power of forgiving sins, much more a standing delegation of this power to any man or order of men, appears in its own nature incommunicable. Almighty God assumes it as his peculiar prerogative; " I even I am he that blotteth out transgression." " And the Lord descended in the cloud and proclaimed the name of the Lord—the Lord God forgiving iniquity, transgression, and sin." As it is repugnant to all our ideas of the Divinity, it is no less inconsistent with our nature and faculties, which cannot possibly extend to a continued knowledge of the thoughts, imaginations, and purposes of others, without which, as hath been observed, in the former section, forgiveness would be the mere exercise of arbitrary power.

IT seems, therefore, more than doubtful, whether the powers committed to Peter, or to the other Apostles, of *binding* and *loosing*, are to be understood of the forgiveness of sin. I do not find one instance in Scripture where the words are used in this sense: nor doth the occasion on which the promise was given seem to lay a

foundation

foundation for such an interpretation.—In the first instance, our Lord being led from Peter's confession to speak of his Church, or the future establishment of Christianity which he should raise upon it, adds, " and I will give thee the keys of the kingdom of heaven, and whatsoever thou shalt bind on earth shall be bound in heaven, and whatsoever thou shalt loose on earth shall be loosed in heaven."—Now what is here that should lead to the idea of forgiving sins? Is it not evident to every reader of the New Testament, that by the kingdom of heaven, in most of Christ's discourses and parables, his Church and Spiritual Kingdom are to be understood? " Go preach, saying, the kingdom of heaven is at hand." By the keys, therefore, of the kingdom of heaven, is plainly meant the stewardship of the mysteries of the Gospel of Christ. This is confirmed by the Apostle's account of his own office, " let a man so account of us as ministers of Christ, and stewards of the mysteries of God." The Apostles were the stewards in Christ's household;—the keys of doctrine, of discipline, and of every Christian institution, were put into their hands; and as they were directed in all things relative to their office by an unerring spirit, whatever they did was approved of by heaven; and, in a particular manner, admitting or rejecting members of Christian communion.

This account is still further supported by a similar promise of our Lord's to his Apostles in general, " whatsoever ye shall bind on earth shall be bound in heaven, and whatsoever ye shall loose on earth shall be loosed in heaven;" where the context plainly indicates

a rea reference to those censures by which the Church of Christ is empowered to reject, and avoid the society of obstinate offenders; "but if he refuse to hear the Church, let him be to thee as a heathen man and a publican;"—as one cut off from the society of the faithful;—and consequently determines the sense of what follows: "Verily, verily, I say unto you, whatsoever ye shall bind on earth shall be bound in heaven, and whatsoever ye shall loose on earth shall be loosed in heaven." This sentence of rejection against an offending brother shall be confirmed or bound upon him in heaven; and, upon his submission and repentence, the sentence being loosed on earth, and he restored again to the privileges of Christianity, it shall be loosed in heaven, and his re-admission receive the divine approbation. This explication appears by no means forced, but to arise from the just connection of the words, and therefore may be properly considered as a key to every similar promise;—such, in particular, as that to the Apostles, "whose sins ye remit, shall be remitted unto them, and whose sins ye retain, they shall be retained."—Nor is the difference of expression material; for that sentence which cut off an obstinate offender from the privileges of Christian communion, bound upon him, beyond all doubt, the sin included in that offence, and for the same reason, restoring him to those privileges, upon repentance, loosed him from this sin.—It doth not appear, therefore, that there were any general powers given even to the Apostles of forgiving sins. There are two considerations which add strength to this conclusion:—That the Apostles did exercise this power of discipline, and their sentence was bound in heaven by the visible interposition

tion of Providence in the *destruction of the flesh*.—They did not exercise this [power of forgiving sins, so far as there appears any evidence from the divine record. They hold up the terms of the Gospel, and call upon men to faith and repentance, leaving the event wholly to God. There is not one instance of an Apostolic absolution in all the New Testament.

But, now, if we should admit that the Apostles were possessed of this power, what is this to Ecclesiastics? Doth it appear that they ever delegated this power to any order of Church Officers? It will, no doubt be answered in the affirmative, and the injunction of the Apostle James will be quoted in proof of it. " Is any man sick among you? let him call for the Elders of the Church, and let them pray over him, anointing him with oil in the name of the Lord, and the prayer of faith shall save the sick, and the Lord shall raise him up, and if he have committed sins they shall be forgiven him." As it must be acknowledged that these words have a plausible appearance, and might be apt to mislead a superficial inquirer, they deserve some notice.

And, *first*, it ought here to be particularly attended to, that the words are wholly confined to the case of sickness. " Is any man *sick*, let him call for the Elders of the Church." This *speciality* puts it beyond all doubt, that the forgiveness spoken of, in the case before us, cannot possibly imply a general and indefinite power committed to those Elders. But, *secondly*, it still remains a question if this *speciality*, even includes in it properly the pardon of sin; or is not rather to be understood in that particular sense in which it occurs in other

parts

parts of scripture, namely, for the recovery of the sick persons; where the cause, by a common figure, is put for the effect.

To explain this, it will be necessary to observe that the Jews entertained a notion that bodily diseases and disorders, as well as signal judgments were the effect of particular sins committed by the person afflicted, or remarkably punished in the order of Providence. "And Jesus answering said unto them, suppose ye that these Galileans were sinners above all other Galileans, because they suffered such things? or these eighteen upon whom the tower of Siloam fell and slew them, think ye that they were sinners above all men that dwelt in Jerusalem? I tell you nay." From this it appears evident what their notions were concerning divine judgments. Again, "And his disciples asked him saying, master, who did sin, this man or his parents that he was born blind? Here it is no less evident that they considered this blindness as the immediate punishment of sin committed either by the man's parents or himself in some pre-existent state, agreeably to the Pythagorean notion with which it would appear our Lord's disciples were tainted. The Pharisees seem to have entertained the same opinion of his case. "They said unto him (the man who had been born blind) thou wast altogether *born in thy sins*, and dost thou teach us? and they cast him out"—To derive weight from their own prejudices, Jesus argues with them in direct conformity to this idea. "When Jesus saw their faith, he saith unto the sick of the palsy, thy sins be forgiven thee: but

there

there were certain of the scribes sitting there, and reasoning in their own hearts, why doth this man thus speak blasphemy? who can forgive sins but God only? And immediately when he perceived in his spirit that they reasoned within themselves, he said unto them why reason ye these things in your hearts? whether is it easier to say to the sick of the palsy, thy sins be forgiven thee, or to say arise take up thy bed and walk? but that ye may know that the Son of Man hath *power to forgive sins*, he saith to the sick of the palsy, *take up thy bed*." From this whole passage it appears with the clearest evidence that by forgiving the sins of the sick of the palsy, our Lord understood healing him, seeing he makes forgiving his sins, and taking up his bed to signify the same thing. Besides, it is evident from the story as narrated by three Evangelists, that this forgiveness did not regard the sick person's sins in general, but those sins which according to the idea of the Jews on this subject, might be considered as the cause of this particular disease: for " when he saw *their* faith"—the faith of those who brought him, " he saith unto the sick of the palsy, thy sins be forgiven thee." But why *thy* sins? It was *their* faith that our Lord saw, and were not *they all* equally sinners who stood in need of pardon? no doubt they were : and the resolution evidently shows that this forgiveness immediately regarded what was peculiar in the case of the sick person—his disease and the cure of it. —This forgiveness, therefore, did not extend to a general pardon, but is by the context and our Lord's particular application restricted to the sick of the palsy taking up his bed.

IT

It may occur to some, perhaps, that Jesus by these words " whether is it easier to say to the sick of the palsy, thy sins be forgiven thee, or to say take up thy bed and walk" intended to point at the absurdity of not admitting, that one who could heal diseases, could likewise pardon sin. But this interpretation cannot be received: because a power of healing diseases, even on some occasions of raising the dead, by no means includes in it a power of pardon. The Jews could have brought examples from their own history of the former, but none of the latter. This argument, therefore, could have had no weight with them. It would have been utterly inconclusive,—so that in every point of view " thy sins be forgiven thee" must be limited to the recovery of the sick person.—From all this we are led, upon the most probable principles, to conclude, that in the text quoted from James, the words, " and if he hath committed any sins they shall be forgiven him" are precisely of the same import with the words that go before, " and the Lord shall raise him up:" and are entirely similar to the expressions of our Lord—" Thy sins be forgiven thee," " Take up thy bed and walk." Both cases are obviously opened by the same key.

But take it in what sense you please, the case is extraordinary, and by no means applicable to the general state of Christianity. Ten thousand rivers of *oil*, and the prayers of all the priests on earth are not sufficient to work one cure of this kind. The cure may be affected in the order of Providence, or by the use of natural means; but they dare not pretend that by anointing with oil and the efficacy of their prayers " the Lord *shall raise* up the sick." And where the effects have ceased, we may demonstratively conclude that the power is no more.

CHAP. X.

OF CHRISTIAN TEACHERS.

SECT. I.

OF THE FOUNDATION ON WHICH THIS CHARACTER RESTS.

THOUGH, in the very introduction to this inquiry, the author, it is hoped, will appear, to the attentive reader, to have precluded every objection against his design as unfriendly to the ministers of religion;—still suspicions may remain with some, that his reasoning is chiefly formed to set aside this order of men altogether, with whom the religious concerns of mankind are so inseparably connected, that, without them, a sense of divine things would quickly languish, if not be wholly erased from the human mind. And it may be asked, by way of ridicule, who these ministers of religion are, by what criterion they are to be distinguished, and for what end they serve? " You have given us to understand, that the claim to Apostolic succession is equally false and presumptuous,—the imposition of *lying priests*; that laying on of hands is a rite neither peculiar to ministerial ordination, nor accompanied with any extraordinary efficacy; that the administration of the sacraments doth not depend on the one, or the other; and that

that all the privileges of the Church of Christ are the privileges of common Christianity, and properly belong to Christian communion.—What order then do these ministers of religion hold, and upon what foundation do they stand? Have all equally a right to be ministers of religion, or what constitutes the difference? Of what importance are they to society, and what is their leading and distinguishing character?"

To these questions he will give the best answer he can, and, he flatters himself, a satisfactory one to those who, void of prepossessions, search for the truth, and are disposed to consult the Scriptures and their own understanding.—And his answer is this: Every one hath not equally a right to be a minister of religion, because every one is neither possessed of the proper qualifications nor call.—That, though this character, in the ordinary dispensations of Providence, stands on the common foundation of religion itself, whether natural or revealed, so far as it is a public institution necessary to promote the happiness of mankind; to limit the administration of the public offices of it to a certain order of men, as a point of order and discipline, in formed religious societies, appears not only useful but necessary.—That the administrator, therefore, of every public religious act in which the society unite, but which, on account of this external order, or to render it a common action, must be performed by one, is a *minister* of religion *authorised* to exert the duties of his office by tacit agreement, in virtue of a plan antecedently established by common edification, or by the immediate and particular choice of a Christian community.

To

To explain this account a little more fully, let it be observed, that there is a wide difference between affirming, that certain rights belong to society as such, and that these rights belong to every individual. The right of magistracy, with all the departments, offices, and forms, that tend to constitute a well regulated state, belong to society, and is one of its natural and essential rights; but it doth not from thence follow, that every man is at liberty to assume the supreme power, or that the many inferior stations, and offices, necessary to compleat the various gradations of civil œconomy, lie at the discretion of every individual: and yet it is certainly true, those cases excepted, where Providence may evidently and signally interpose, antecedently to the choice of the community, or independently of their consent, tacit or expressed; no man possesses a preference but what arises from considerations of superior wisdom, courage, virtue, or, in general, some one talent of being more extensively useful; and even these are qualities of which he is not to state himself a judge: the society, either by the majority of voices, or some established plan of procedure, are the final judges, and can alone vest him with the proper authority.—The same reasoning holds exactly in religion, with regard to administration, precedency, and every public and social duty performed in the name of the society, which must be transferred to one, and may be transferred without hurting the personal rights of individuals:—Rights which were antecedently common, so that no one, by any positive law, could claim a preference, by all the laws of decency, propriety, and reason, may be transferred from the many to one, who from that moment acts by lawful authority; by a right that may properly be called his own; becaufe, while it remains in him, he poffeffes the power of the fociety, and the fociety act by him.

As the common right which the fociety thus transfer conftitutes this public right,—it is divine; for the rights of the fociety, whether civil or religious, being a part of the divine inftitution, either natural or moral, whoever is empowered by them, holds a truft from God: he is the minifter of God for their good, while he is engaged in the faithful difcharge of it. But he holds no exclufive right;—no fociety being at liberty to entruft powers for the public good or edification, which they are not authorifed, and ought not, to recal when they ceafe to anfwer that end; when he or they who receive the truft, become unworthy of it, or incapable of difcharging it.—The all-wife and all-gracious Lord, in the conftitution of his government, confults the general happinefs of his rational creation,—if they would only learn to confult their own. He gives to no mortal a power which they may abufe without controul, at the expence of the civil or religious rights of mankind. If they will wantonly throw away their own rights, they muft fuffer for their folly, and are accountable to him.

There is one thing, however, that ought to be carefully attended to in this illuftration from civil government—That, as members of civil fociety, our wants, whether real or artificial, being more various, our relations and dependence more diverfified, and the objects of our purfuits, and the gratification of our paffions
interfering

interfering more with one another—political government doth not eafily admit of little focieties chequered into one another, and regulated by different laws and modes of adminiftration. Such focieties would naturally ufurp upon one another, till fuperior policy or power had enabled one or more to fubject the reft to their jurifdiction, to extend their boundaries, and to eftablifh a more general fyftem of laws. Thus civil fociety would go on by new acceffions of dominion, forming itfelf into larger diftricts and ftates, till a reciprocal jealoufy had taken place, and formed a political balance fufficient to preferve the weak from falling a facrifice to the more powerful; fo that it fhould become difficult or hazardous to attempt further encroachments. But with regard to religious concerns the cafe becomes quite different, as hath in part been explained (Chap 3d.) The number of focieties differing from one another, or the number of which thofe focieties are compofed makes no difference *here*; becaufe in fact they have no more dependence upon one another than a Briton hath upon a Californian. Nothing but a fpirit of *prieftcraft* and ecclefiaftic ufurpation could lead any one in religious concerns, to oppofe, or give the fmalleft difturbance to another. While men differ in opinions, which, without doing violence to our rational faculties, can never become uniform, as they are fuppofed to aim at the fame common end, they ought to bear with one another, and to love one another—No doubt, if our views were more extenfive, our inquiries more impartial, and our prejudices and paffions lefs violent; if education and particular circumftances, which it were difficult to explain, did not confpire to pervert our underftandings, and obftruct the knowlege

of

of the truth, the system of christians would be more uniform, and more consistent—And a happy time may come when all men shall be of " one heart and of one mind in the Lord:" but till such a wished for period, all the external order in religion that ought to be looked for is, that every christian community, professing to unite in common principles, act consistently with themselves, consistently with the order of society, and without assuming a dominion over the consciences of others.

It will possibly be urged by some even who imagine they are free from every tincture of priestcraft—That it would be absurd to constitute those who themselves stand in need of teaching, judges of their own teachers. In answer to this, it is asked, doth civil government suppose every individual possessed of talents capable of judging with propriety of the qualifications of the Supreme Magistrate? Certainly: yet upon the principles of real liberty, and agreeably to the unalienable rights of human nature, it ought not to be departed from, that this right doth remain in the collective body, and that those who discharge the office of magistracy exert every power in virtue of it either formally, or virtually ceded to them. Every recession from this capital point is a step towards civil tyranny—The argument is entirely similar with regard to public teachers. Though individuals may be incompetent judges of the qualifications necessary for the discharge of this office; in every christian community in their collective capacity, their is a right, however they may abuse it, of chusing a public, teacher in the exercise of which they may act as appears most subservient to the ends of order and edification.

If

If they have not this right, to whom doth it belong? Who hath a power over their consciences, to controul their choice, and say you shall not be directed by your own judgment? Human laws have no jurisdiction here, and if there be any divine law that restrains our christian liberty let it be pointed out—Besides, as in every civil society there are always some of superior abilities and wisdom, who, without aiming at authority, or assuming over the understandings of others, acquire respect and influence, and are consulted on every important event, so that they may be said to direct the majority, though voluntarily and by their own choice; it will seldom, if ever, happen, that in a religious community there are not likewise a few who, by their distinguished knowlege and piety, have acquired a general confidence, and by whom the society chuse to act.

There is one consideration still behind that entirely removes this objection—That vesting a christian society with the power of election, doth not state them as absolute judges of qualifications antecedently: because, in every christian community, where there is any sense of propriety and fitness, besides general rules, agreeably to which alone, one can assume the character of a public teacher—certain judges are appointed, by the very constitution of the society, who, in the last instance take trial of the qualifications of candidates. This hath been the manner, and probably will continue to be the manner in all well-regulated christian societies. And it will no doubt happen that, according to the strict observance of those rules, and the capacity, piety, and attention of those judges, licentiates for the ministry will

will be more or less deserving and useful—But it ought to be carefully observed, that qualifications are one thing, and a right to preside in a christian society quite another, (see Chap. 5. Sect. 3.) These two ought never to be confounded—and in this lies the great secret of christian liberty.

It is not meant, by any thing here suggested, that the civil government hath not a right to establish a religious polity so far, as its public institutions do not appear inconsistent with the genius of christianity in general, or any divine law in particular; that agreeably to this they may not appoint ministers properly qualified, with benefices as public rewards of their labours. But in doing of this, every wise state will consult the dispositions and religious opinions of a people, if these are not hurtful to good order, and the principles on which the civil constitution rests—The reason is obvious: the more the people are knit to the religious establishment, their political affections, and their attachments to religion, and its ministers will be insensibly blended together, and become the joint security and strength of the state. But if the ministers of the constitution shall become merely nominal; if the people are wholly alienated from them, their opinions, their mode of government and worship; as the benefices, originally intended to reward talents employed for the promotion of virtue and public happiness, will remain in the hands of those who contribute nothing to either—the state, at the same time, will become more feeble by losing one effectual handle of managing the people: for a mere protection of the civil powers, though in itself a great blessing, will not operate so powerfully on the affections

ons as the security of an establishment, and the sweets of a public reward. Whatever measures, therefore a state may be engaged to adopt, that drives the bulk of its subjects from the public teachers to look out for ministers of their own, will be found in the issue, to be, at best, but bad policy—nor can it possibly reflect honour on the public teachers themselves to be deserted by the whole body the people, and to hold the public rewards while they contribute nothing to the public good. If ever this should happen, it would be such a prostitution of the public funds, as would not be long tolerated under good government.—The nominal teachers would, inevitably, in the issue, fall a sacrifice. The same policy that dictated the original establishment, would naturally be directed to throw the public rewards into the hands of those who had acquired the affections of the people: it being undoubtedly the wisdom of government to ease the public of a tax, not only consistently with the interest of the state, but evidently subservient to it.—But, if instead of a public establishment, whereby a certain order of public teachers are supported and encouraged, at the same time that the people are left to their own choice, the state should, at any time, by penal laws, pretend to bind the people to the ministry of certain pastors, to whom a particular district is committed:—the consequence must infallibly be, the total subversion of civil and religious liberty, or the recovery of both, by some important revolution in government.

SECT. II.

Of the Importance of the Character of a Public Teacher.

THE importance of any inftitution to mankind is to be eftimated from the nature and tendency of the end it is defigned to promote, and from its immediate and neceffary connection with that end. If the end is of no real or lafting benefit to public or private happinefs, fhould the means appear the beft that have been yet devifed, the human underftanding, however, feemingly ingenioufly employed, and whatever ardor or zeal it may manifeft, is, at beft, but entertained about trifles, which may occupy and amufe little minds, but can never fhow its real vigour and ufefulnefs.—But if the end is confeffedly of great importance, the only inquiry is, how far the means are neceffary and adequate to it. The firft queftion, therefore, comes to be, whether Chriftianity is of real importance to mankind? A queftion that will be readily anfwered in the affirmative: for however men may have been led to differ in their accounts of the Chriftian Religion, arifing from the different iffue of their own inquiries, but more frequently from the different reprefentations that theologians have given of it; it may be affirmed, in the general, that no real friend to natural religion, and to thofe duties on which the happinefs of fociety, and our hopes as reafonable and accountable creatures depend, but muft of neceffity admit, that the Religion of Chrift contains in it a fyftem of moral duties immediately arifing from our

relation

relation to one another, and our relation to the great Author of our exiſtence, more plain, more perfect, and more adapted to the feelings of the human mind than any other yet made known to the world. It is not my purpoſe, however, to enter into this argument at preſent. There is no occaſion for touching upon it, but as it introduces the next queſtion by which this part of our ſubject is chiefly illuſtrated.

If Chriſtianity is of real importance to mankind, whether it is, of itſelf, poſſeſſed of internal powers to work its own way, and gain upon the minds of men without any ſubſidiary aids—without the aids of preaching and public inſtruction? To this it will, perhaps, be anſwered by ſome, that it certainly is poſſeſſed of ſuch powers; that to ſuppoſe otherwiſe would neceſſarily throw this reflection on its Divine Author—that he either wanted the power or the will to give execution to his own plan. But ſuch an anſwer, we apprehend, ought by no means to be admitted. Neither the plainneſs nor importance of the principles or precepts of Chriſtianity are ſufficient to preſerve them from corruption and decay, being totally perverted, or wholly overlooked, without a continued energy of Divine Power ſufficient to fix the attention, and counterwork the prejudices of the human mind. Nothing could have been more ſimple and obvious, we are naturally led to think, than the original law of nature. It was doubtleſs, the tranſcript of the Divinity on the mind of man: the intimations of his will in legible characters written upon his conſcience: yet this original ſignature itſelf proved inſufficient to preſerve clear and permanent impreſſions.

In

In order, therefore, to restore and enforce a sense of natural religion, and original obligation, God raised up an eminent preacher of righteousness to the antediluvian world, and afterwards Abraham to whom he made himself known. And, in different periods, signal and illustrious preachers and patterns of virtue have appeared as light shining in a dark place: but being neither vested with any public authority, or wholly purified themselves from gross errors in speculation, nor sufficiently fortified against giving way to prevailing idolatry and superstition in practice—their lectures too refined, and little adapted to vulgar understandings, were attended with no lasting benefit. Or if they were retained in the closets of a few select philosophers, their professed scholars or admirers, and who endeavoured to improve upon them, they became still more raised above the ordinary comprehension, by being wholly converted into an abstract science little connected with the feelings of the human heart. Some exceptions there are—men of attention to the human frame, and to the state of man, and whose writings, no doubt, have been of great service in preserving a sense of Deity and Morals. These were the ministers of natural religion, raised up to preserve the world from total corruption and darkness. It may be thought, perhaps, that the small influence of natural religion hath been chiefly owing to its not having been committed to writing; that, through the strength of the passions, and the unavoidable effect of sensible objects upon the mind, the strongest impressions wear out; and, through the imperfection of tradition, the clearest discoveries are lost; but that the Christian Religion is exposed to none of these draw-backs: it
having

having been committed to writing by the Evangelists and Apostles themselves, and from the period of its publication having remained a standing and authenticated record: and more especially, by the discovery of the art of printing, among other important advantages, it having been widely diffused, and put into the hands of almost every individual. All this must be acknowledged; and that in these respects Christianity hath evidently the advantage of the religion of nature, whether we ascribe its origin to revelation, or certain radical impressions upon the human mind. An authentic public record remains a standard to which we can appeal, and, amidst the greatest ignorance and perversion, may prove the means of recovering the knowledge of the truth, by enabling us to separate with certainty between it, and those errors that seem twisted with it, or grafted into it —or maintained in direct opposition. This effect it is fitted to produce, it hath often produced in a lesser degree, but in our reformation from popery in a signal manner. If Ecclesiastics, after establishing their heterogeneous system of Paganism and Christianity, so politically blended together, and so artfully contrived to ensnare the consciences of mankind, had been able to have destroyed the original record, so that not one copy of it should have remained, nor any thing further of its contents than was to be gathered from public articles, and the decisions of councils; they might at this day have been absolute Lords of Europe, with the honour of being the priests of a theology, the most extraordinary that ever human invention put together. The Scriptures, therefore, by being a permanent and uniform standard, it must be acknowledged, become of more general and lasting benefit than the most perfect system of natural religion; but it is evident, from the amazing encroachments of the Church of Rome, from the unscriptural tenets of many Protestants, from the opposite and contradictory systems of different religious sects, some of which are replete with the wildest enthusiasm, and the grossest conceptions of the deity, that they are by no means an absolute security against abuse.

But how far is public instruction fitted to prevent this effect? This is the capital point. And it is urged on the negative;—That public teaching is the very source of the evil of which we complain, and, therefore, can never prove the cure of it;—That hereby the vanity of the preacher is gratified in displaying his own talents, and propagating his own opinions;—That from this abuse of the pulpit have sprung those endless sects, and all that diversity and opposition of sentiments that have exposed the cause of Christianity and weakened its credit;—That the only teaching allowable, is reading the Scriptures in public without any comment, leaving them to their free course and operation;—That this, therefore, with the other public offices of religion, should constitute the whole work of a minister. This may appear to some highly plausible, and, therefore, deserves some consideration. I beg leave to offer a few remarks upon it.

And, *first*, I would observe, that supposing this originally would have been a wise and necessary institution; that such a regulation, universally established, and faithfully adhered to, from the commencement of Christianity

Christianity downwards, would have prevented the rise of all those sects and opinions that have unhappily divided, and still divide the Christian world ;—it is now too late. What is a proper security against an evil, and what is necessary to counteract its effects, are things totally distinct. Could you bring all Christendom to agree in setting aside public teaching, and confining ministers to simple reading of the Scriptures, which, I apprehend, would be a matter of some difficulty,—the evil is already spread ; already hath the human mind exhausted all its wildness and luxuriancy both in broaching and propagating opinions. The question, therefore, is not whether public teaching ought to have been originally admitted as an institution fitted for the advancement of Christianity ; but whether it is now necessary ? whether errors, propagated publicly, ought not to be publicly guarded against and exposed ? Besides, this argument, if it is of any weight, goes too far, and upon the same foundation must condemn every commentary on the Scriptures, and all writings on religion : for, beyond all doubt, if these are allowable ; if it serve, in any point of view, the interests of Virtue and Christianity, to explain the sacred volume, to reason, to admonish, and to employ all the arts of human eloquence to enforce the several doctrines and precepts of religion ; it is no less proper to explain the Scriptures and to preach in public.—It were surely in the highest degree absurd to permit the one and restrain the other.—" But thousands hear that never read, and speak pertinently in public who never write books ; and, therefore, in the one case more mischief may be done than in the other." True ; but let it be remembered,—more good too.

too. A public teacher may often do more service by a pertinent and seasonable reflection, a happy illustration, a well judged address, than an ingenious and learned author by a volume. This manner of enlightening the understanding, and touching the heart is always at hand; and, where the preacher is a man who hath acquired that authority which propriety of manners, and a real attention to the best interests of a Christian Society never fail to produce, is attended with a force and influence which the best writer is incapable of. A few knowing faithful public teachers of just and liberal sentiments, experimentally acquainted with vital religion, and the genuine fervors of rational devotion, can be of more real service to the cause of truth and virtue than a thousand authors.

But, *secondly*, it is extremely doubtful whether such a plan would answer the end in view. For if you should never explain the Scriptures, nor attempt public instruction of any kind, you cannot prevent the human mind from thinking, from speaking, from reasoning on the Scriptures and Religion. It is too inquisitive. The subject is too interesting. And if men think, speak, and reason, they will differ in opinions, and each will find its peculiar votaries. Perhaps never was an opinion broached where one stood single. Sects will, therefore, arise. Pride and arrogance, on one side, will give the provocation and proclaim the war; zeal perhaps for the truth, or a spirit roused by opposition and asperity, will engage the other, and thus hostilities will commence. This will give the alarm to others, who never thought of calling in question the established opinions: a spirit of

CHAP. X. OF CHRISTIAN TEACHERS.

of inquiry will be awakened, and in attempting to discover on which side the truth lies, new avenues will open: so that without supposing a state that never existed, so far as I know, it would be impossible that the Scriptures should be in every body's hands, and read publicly every week, without thinking about them, and judging what particular system of religion they contained. In a country of liberty, men would speak their sentiments with freedom, they would dispute, they would write, they would print. Nor would all the terrors of popish inquisition wholly restrain this impulse of the human mind. One would have thought, when the Ecclesiastic monarchy of the papal chair had arrived at such absolute dominion, that the kings of the earth trembled at its nod, that no one would have been bold enough to differ publicly from the established superstition;—but there is in some minds an enthusiasm, a delusion arising from false notions of superior communications, and in others, a curiosity and innate love of the truth, with a vigour of spirit utterly unconquerable, and that will dare to break through every restraint: the most despotic and unrelenting exercise, therefore, of Ecclesiastic tyranny produce instances of both these; and by the secret, though slow and distant operation of the last, were the reformers enabled to assert their own cause, and vindicate the common rights of humanity. Was this, may we ask, owing to the vanity of public teachers in broaching new fangled opinions?—If it was, it may be pronounced to be one happy effect of it, that ought to recommend this institution to all the friends of civil and religious liberty, and render it venerable to the end of the world.

But, if by superseding public instruction, the growth of what is called sectarism, and the spreading of different opinions should be prevented, what would be the consequence? An established system would prevail,—not the Scriptures: for they will never become an established system, but on such general terms as leaves every body to think for himself, and to be directed by his own opinions and mode of worship:—but a system fabricated by Ecclesiastics, who, taking the advantage of this restraint laid upon public instruction, would gain an unlimited ascendance over the mind; and thus the truth would remain more obscured than amidst all the variety of opinions that ever have been, or will be broached. If you do not, somewhere, open an avenue to the truth, as a balance to the best establishment in religion, or the most perfect human system that ever was yet formed, you at once injure the cause of christianity and religious liberty, and put into the hands of men, a power which, experience leaves us no room to doubt, that they will certainly abuse.—And what can more fairly promise success than public teaching, exempted from the terror of penal laws, and enjoying the immunities of a free constitution? What could be a more effectual antidote against the poison of established error? What could more effectually curb the insolence, or check the encroachments of established Ecclesiastics? No one would pretend to substitute human decisions in place of the Scriptures, or human authority in the place of evidence. The body of the people, accustomed to free and candid disquisition, would learn to think, and to vindicate the rights of their reasonable natures; and it would become equally difficult to render them the dupes of civil or Ecclesiastic fiaftic ufurpation. Such a degree of knowledge, and such a fenfe of freedom, would be equally hateful and offenfive to priefts and tyrants: but they are the glory and pride of Great Britain, encouraged by our conftitution, and the fupport of it;—the honour of the great body of our clergy, and daily encreafed and confirmed by them.

But befides explaining the Scriptures, and promoting the caufe of truth and religious liberty, there are other great and important advantages that arife from this inftitution. Every one may be fufficiently convinced, from his own experience, that religious confiderations, however in theory they may be acknowledged worthy to occupy our moft ferious attention, and of the higheft moment to our real happinefs, are by no means the objects generally entertained, and on which the mind delights to dwell and employ itfelf. Our convictions concerning the moft important truths, and the impreffions they leave upon the mind, are evidently occafional and momentary; or if they continue for a longer fpace, they gradually lofe their force and wear off, till amidft objects that daily furround us, and folicit our attention from more immediate views, we lofe fight of them altogether.—Men often come to contrive expedients, and to invent ingenious excufes to fatisfy themfelves amidft the moft criminal inattention to every thing ferious, without once attempting to balance the confiftency of their prefent conduct and future hopes. It can, therefore, admit of no doubt, that the inattention of the generality to religious concerns, amidft that diffipation of mind which evidently prevails, amidft the various pursuits of riches, pleasure, and ambition, that seem to engross every affection, and to captivate every power of the soul, public teaching must be, in the highest degree, necessary. In such a situation there is, surely, great need of having divine things brought often under our review, and urged home upon the conscience by every possible argument. There is great need of daily monitors, by whose friendly and seasonable aid, secure and thoughtless minds, if possible may be alarmed, and brought to fix upon themselves, and their eternal concerns; and that those who have been seduced from the paths of virtue, may be brought back again to their first convictions, and the original impressions they had felt be recovered, improved, and confirmed;—for this purpose a public teacher of any talents hath a great advantage. While he describes characters, while he reproves vice in general, he may draw such striking outlines, features so strong and lively, as, however seemingly distant and concealed, will necessarily, on many occasions, exhibit ones own picture to himself, without alarming his pride;—he may pierce the conscience without awakening resentments against the hand that levelled the weapon. And which is no inconsiderable part of his office, by a proper representation, by a pertinent application of his subject, he may administer seasonable medicine to the mind oppressed by calamity, or disquieted by a sense of guilt;—while it is yet tender and susceptible, and every avenue lies open, what heartfelt lectures may he not read, what consolations may he not pour into the soul, what reviving hopes, what animated views may he not lay open? " The words of the wise are gracious, and pleasant words like the honey comb."

comb."—God himself condescends to comfort those that are cast down, and hath given it in commission to his ministers to comfort his people;—" to strengthen the weak hands, and to confirm the feeble knees, and to say to them that are of a fearful heart, fear not, be strong."—A minister, therefore, if fitted to discharge this part of his work with tenderness and capacity, does honour to his character, and is a blessing to his people.

There is another consideration on this subject that arises from the unavoidable circumstances in which the far greater part of mankind are placed—They are engaged in one continued struggle amidst the embarrassments and cares of life. They enter early into toil and laborious exercise for their daily bread, which naturally contracts the intellectual faculties. Their whole time and attention are occupied in providing for their own bodily wants, or in furnishing necessary support and provision for their families. The little instruction they had received while children hath left but confused and imperfect traces upon their minds, which their daily and necessary engagements are apt entirely to deface—In such circumstances were it not for the advantage of public instruction, it may be affirmed, that they would lose religious impressions altogether, and generate into a state of downright barbarism.—But is not private instruction a more successful method of promoting religious knowlege? If it should, it is a method exposed to every objection that can be offered against public instruction: because, if a minister have access to instruct his people in private, he may explain the scriptures to them, and propagate his own opinions among them; you must, therefore,

exclude

exclude private as well as public teaching, or confine both equally to reading the fcriptures. But the fact is, that private teaching though highly proper, is not equally fitted for general edification with public: no teacher being able to repeat to a number of different little focieties what he can do weekly to one. Here all are taught at the fame expence to the teacher, and the fame profit to the hearer, if the fpeaker eqnally aims at inftruction. The one, however, is not intended to fuperfede the other: both operate towards the fame end, and are no lefs the duty of the minifters of religion.

But in every inquiry of this kind, it will be faid, that the only way to arrive at any probable conclufion is, to appeal to experience. What good hath this inftitution done for near eighteen hundred years paft? Is not the ignorance to be found among the greater part of thofe who attend upon public teaching, even of the plaineft doctrines of Chriftianity almoft incredible, where this inftitution hath obtained, and been continued from generation to generation? Their notions of God are at beft but a confufed medley of fuperftion and enthufiafm, with fome unintelligible jargon of fyftematic divinity; fo that you would be tempted to think that natural religion had been entirely left out of the queftion. Where then are the effects of this inftitution? Of what benefit hath it been for promoting knowledge and virtue? I am well difpofed to admit the force of this objection fo far as to acknowlege, that—where the corruptions and abominable fuperftitions introduced by *priefts*, and which have been propagated with fuch aftonifhing fuccefs, have been fubftituted and taught in the place of genuine

Chriftianity

Christianity—a greater perversion hath followed than could have arisen from the total suppression of this institution: as it may be affirmed without violating the laws of truth and charity, that no species of religion, so far as we know, professed among the most barbarous nations, hath yet equalled the system of priestcraft that prevailed in Christendom for many centuries—originally bottomed on the tenets which have been the subject of this inquiry, and which every *priest*, in circumstances that would permit them to operate in all their latitude, would infallibly re-establish. And in the general it ought to be admitted, that if public teachers had been at more pains to understand and explain the religion of Christ,—had been more disengaged from the prejudices of established creeds, from a spirit of ambition, from pride and party views,—had been more honest, and more attentive to the great duties of their office, their hearers would have been more intelligent, more rational, and better Christians. But may not an institution be excellent, and highly beneficial in itself, though neglected, or even abused and perverted from its original purpose? If the abuse of an institution were a good argument against it, it is difficult to say what institutions ought to be preserved among mankind. Christianity, natural religion, and civil government, would be banished from the world together. No reasoning, therefore, can be more unjust. The very abuse may show the necessity, not of abolishing the institution, but of restoring it to its original intention and purity. The more that *priests* have poisoned the fountains of knowledge and virtue, of the greater importance to the happiness of mankind must intelligent, humble, and faithful

teachers

teachers be. If Christianity hath been perverted by the designs of Ecclesiastics who have had a distinct trade — a political fabric of their own to establish; let it be restored again to its primitive simplicity by men who derive their character from their work, and their importance from the choice of those who are satisfied — that they deserve it.

But, setting aside the gross superstitions and total perversion of the human faculties by a false system of religion — it is to be hoped, that, even amidst many errors, this institution hath been attended with happy effects on the morals of mankind. Before we can possibly affirm the contrary, we must state a case where Christianity hath been professed without the aids of this institution: if such a case could be found, and it could be fairly made appear that the same measure of religious knowledge, the same measure of private and public virtue, of civil and moral order hath obtained, it must be admitted, that, from such a comparative view, no feeble presumption would arise against what hath been urged on this subject. But it is presumed, that no such instance can be produced.—And we can state another comparative view, that gives all the satisfaction on this article that is necessary;—that, where other circumstances are supposed to be equal, the superior knowledge, piety, and assiduous labours of a minister among his people, seldom fail to be distinguished, if he hath continued any time among them —— In the lowest view, if public teaching hath not improved the religious knowledge, and manners of mankind, to any considerable degree, may it not be modestly affirmed that it hath preserved them

them from growing worfe? And this, could no more be faid, would render this inftitution a public benefit of no fmall account. But if ever it fhall be attended with remarkable fuccefs, it muft be entirely left to the divine bleffing unreftrained by creeds, or articles, or conditions of any kind — but the Bible, public order and decency.

And now, reader, having finifhed this little work, and difcharged what I thought my duty to the public, I turn myfelf, in conclufion, to another quarter.

" O thou eternal fountain of light, to whom is known the purity of my intentions in what I have, in thefe pages, committed to paper, accept, I befeech thee, of this humble tribute I would offer up unto thee,—intended to expofe, what hath always appeared to me, the prefumptuous claims of men to powers which thou haft committed to no mortal. If thefe arrogant pretenders are under the influence of an erroneous confcience, and have been betrayed by the weaknefs of their own underftandings, let the light penetrate their hearts, and break through prejudices more obftinate than adamant. If a fpirit of pride, if defigning and ambitious views have firft led them afide, and brought them, in the iffue, to impofe upon themfelves, or have rendered them unwilling to acknowledge the truth, and to undeceive the credulous, fuperftitious multitude;—fmite this pride to the earth, let thefe ambitious views appear in their natural odious light, as a bafe ufurpation of thy facred prerogative; and difpofe them to glorify thee by an ingenuous and open confeffion. But if the writer himfelf, after his beft inquiries, fhould be

the

the person misled by prejudices, and who hath, in any instance, departed from the truth; if he hath dropt the most distant hint injurious to the important doctrines of Christianity, the spiritual kingdom of thy Son, or the character of his faithful and humble ministers,—out of thine abundant goodness proclaimed in the gospel of peace, and on which he desires to rest all his hopes, do thou forgive thy erring mistaken servant,—but let his labours perish."

FINIS.

www.ingramcontent.com/pod-product-compliance
Lightning Source LLC
Chambersburg PA
CBHW032133230426
43672CB00011B/2317